Kneeling Before Corn

biodiversity in small spaces

Virginia D. Nazarea, Series Editor

KNEELING CORN BEFORE

Recuperating More-than-Human Intimacies on the Salvadoran Milpa

**MIKE ANASTARIO,
ELENA SALAMANCA,
AND ELIZABETH HAWKINS**

THE UNIVERSITY OF
ARIZONA PRESS
TUCSON

The University of Arizona Press
www.uapress.arizona.edu

We respectfully acknowledge the University of Arizona is on the land and territories of Indigenous peoples. Today, Arizona is home to twenty-two federally recognized tribes, with Tucson being home to the O'odham and the Yaqui. Committed to diversity and inclusion, the University strives to build sustainable relationships with sovereign Native Nations and Indigenous communities through education offerings, partnerships, and community service.

ISBN-13: 978-0-8165-5337-2 (hardcover)
ISBN-13: 978-0-8165-5338-9 (ebook)

Cover design by Leigh McDonald
Cover art: "Hombre de maíz" (2020), Wilber Salguero
Typeset by Sara Thaxton in 10/14 Warnock Pro with Citrus Gothic Rough and Los Feliz OT

Unless otherwise noted, all photos are by Mike Anastario.

Library of Congress Cataloging-in-Publication Data
Names: Anastario, Mike, 1981– author. | Salamanca, Elena, 1982– author. | Hawkins, Elizabeth, 1983– author.
Title: Kneeling before corn : recuperating more-than-human intimacies on the Salvadoran milpa / Mike Anastario, Elena Salamanca, and Elizabeth Hawkins.
Other titles: Biodiversity in small spaces.
Description: Tucson : University of Arizona Press, 2024. | Series: Biodiversity in small spaces | Includes bibliographical references and index.
Identifiers: LCCN 2023036609 (print) | LCCN 2023036610 (ebook) | ISBN 9780816553372 (paperback) | ISBN 9780816553389 (ebook)
Subjects: LCSH: Human-plant relationships—El Salvador. | Subsistence farming—El Salvador.
Classification: LCC QK46.5.H85 A53 2024 (print) | LCC QK46.5.H85 (ebook) | DDC 306.3/49097284—dc23/eng/20231212
LC record available at https://lccn.loc.gov/2023036609
LC ebook record available at https://lccn.loc.gov/2023036610

Printed in the United States of America
♾ This paper meets the requirements of ANSI/NISO Z39.48-1992 (Permanence of Paper).

CONTENTS

Kneeling Before Corn

Introduction

> We're on our way, dear grandmother. We're just giving you
> instructions. So here is the sign of our word. We'll leave it with
> you. Each of us will plant an ear of green corn. We'll plant them
> in the center of our house. When the corn dries up, this will
> be a sign of our death:
> "Perhaps they died," you'll say, when it dries up. And when
> the sprouting comes:
> "Perhaps they live," you'll say, our dear grandmother and
> mother. From now on, this is the sign of our word.
>
> —XBALANQUE AND HUNAHPU, *THE POPOL VUH*

Chepe's Milpita

"¡Ah este palo hijueputa ya no, si no vas a dar ya te voy a meter el hacha! le
digo . . . de repente ya tiene un mango ahí."

Reclined in a hammock at dusk, Chepe explains how he verbally threat-
ened a mango tree to make it grow fruit. He first insulted the tree (calling it
a "sonofabitch") and then gave it a death threat: "If you're not going to give
me anything, then I'm going to stick an axe in you!" Chepe pauses to let
those words sink in before concluding that the tree subsequently produced
a mango.

These words that get a stubborn tree to bear fruit are a form of interspecies communication told to other people in a story about a past that involves
a nonhuman and a human. In this temporal interplay, a lesson emerges for
the listener. Chepe clarifies that the words are indeed a threat to the plant's
life, but the words are also a bluff ("O sea lo salvequeo ¡vea pues!"). The point
is to get the plant to produce fruit, which the plant might not need to do at
this point in its life cycle but which the people who live under and near the
tree want it to do. Chepe has a peaceful demeanor and speaks rural Chalateco Spanish in what sounds like an endless sigh. It is difficult to imagine
him killing anything. It is all the more chilling to hear him talk like this in a
space that holds the memory of a bloody civil war and where death arrives

too early for so many beings within this rural place. Memories of a rural past are woven into Chepe's narrative style of instruction. Chepe learned how to make plants grow from family members who are now dead, and he will impart this wisdom to family, students, and researchers who will listen.

Chepe grew up in the northern part of El Salvador, near the Honduran border. He did not own shoes until he was a teenager. He learned to farm from his father, who would wake up before first light to stare at the stars and evaluate the cloud formations in an ever-changing sky. Multiple signals in the sensorium at dawn helped Chepe's father predict the rain. Chepe remembers how the farmers of his parents' generation understood the signals. He sees rural children's attention divested by smartphones that lure them to faraway places where they forget the secrets, memories, and ways of this rural place. Most of Chepe's children will emigrate by the time this book is published. Chepe deposits remnants of knowledge into the tape recorder. This time, it is about what he recently said to the avocado tree outside his house:

> "Ahí parado ¡va!, si no se te queda nada . . . tengo la motosierra." Tres tiene, aguacates tiene por ahí.

> "Alright then, if you don't have anything left . . . I have a chainsaw." Now the tree has three avocados.

Chepe will eventually walk those of us who record his words to the avocado tree. As Chepe walks, he moves through something that is like a home garden. It is his *milpita* (little milpa), a small "replica" of a larger milpa that Chepe used to farm when he was younger. A milpa is a type of subsistence farm where corn, beans, squash, and other varieties of plants and fruit are grown. Milpas can occupy the most unlikely spaces. They cover large swaths of mountainous terrain; they appear in the home gardens of rural Salvadorans, in small plots of land outside homes in the urban capital, in medians between highway roads, alongside parking lots tended to by guards, between sidewalks, and in dedicated plots of well-manicured backyards of Salvadoran migrants living in the suburban United States. Chepe's milpita is a place where *caña rayada* (striped sugarcane), *caña de seda* (silk sugarcane), and *piña india* (Indian pineapple) grow. He saves and gifts them to people each year. He claims that these varieties were forgotten with the growth of monocrops in El Salvador. The sugarcane, pineapple, and fruit trees are easy to miss because they are peripheral to the *maíz blanco* (white corn) and *maíz negro* (black corn) growing strong in human-made patterns under direct sunlight near Chepe's house. The corncobs will be spotted, reflecting Chepe's practice of open pollination. About four weeks after the corn has sprouted, it will signal to Chepe, through growth and color, that it needs fertilizer. Chepe will burn *leña* (firewood) to produce ash that he will mix with ammonium sulphate and a nitrogen/phosphorous/potassium fertilizer combination.

For a while, Chepe had forgotten about using ash to fertilize corn. As a Chalateco child in the 1950s, Chepe burned down delimited sections of the forest with his father. The thick layer of ash that fell upon the topsoil piled up like black snow, and the traditional corn varieties that they planted burst out of the earth without the use of agrichemicals. After so many changes to the agrarian lifeway, Chepe learned to use synthetic fertilizers on the same plot of land, overused and overfertilized in this new way of working in the world, and all but forgot about the power of ash to fertilize corn. One of Chepe's friends reminded him about the ash, and he has gone back to mixing what he once knew (fire and fallow farming) with what he now knows about modern agricultural science to reproduce his milpita each year.

It is easy for a visitor to miss, but there is a single shoot of corn growing from a small pot in front of Chepe's house. It is recognizably a corn stalk, but it is small and undernourished. An overzealous ethnographer might get tempted to assign more significance to that single shoot of corn than should probably be assigned to it. There is always a backstory for growing plants, but Chepe is such a kind host that he will defer his voice to that of an "educated" outsider who may have an alternative explanation for the way he lives his life. This is why it is so important to just listen, even when the stories go on for hours. This is why it is important to have hours to spend with Chepe, lying around in hammocks, taking notes and tours, and recording Chepe after listening to stories that begin, with time, to repeat themselves. Ethnography takes time. If we approach Chepe with a spirit of curiosity and ask him about that single shoot of corn, he explains that it is the experimental seed he used to test the batch of seeds for sowing his milpita. His test produced a signal that announces the life in the milpa beside it, even as the small plant withers close to death. Its life and death are visible to all who visit Chepe's house this rainy season.

Chepe's milpita is small, unruly, and private. It is a laboratory and a space that materializes what Chepe narrates amid the growing rows of corn that will be used to make nixtamalized tortillas, *pupusas* (corn pancakes stuffed with beans, cheese, and other ingredients), and atole. His intimate forms of communication with and attunements to the plants, as well as his memories of plants, are the focus of our studies, as are the ways in which these intimacies move away from Chepe's plants and through the people connected to Chepe. This includes the people who interview Chepe and the way that they are moved into actions by the plants around him and his ideas, re-turning his stories of previous rainy seasons and plant growth in the rural north of El Salvador.

Core Concepts

The cultivation of the three sisters—corn, beans, and squash—on subsistence farms in El Salvador is a multispecies, world-making, ongoing process. *Milpa* is the word that is used to describe a small subsistence corn farm. It is derived from the word *milli* (field, or a piece of land under active cultivation) in Nahuatl (Pizzigoni 2007; Sellen 2011; Harrison 2007, 71). It is a farming practice that uses perennial, intercropping, and swidden (fire and fallow) techniques, and that predates the Spanish conquest of the Americas (González 2001, 161; Ford and Nigh 2015). The word *milpa* is both a linguistic syncretism and an encoding device, drawing in multiple species with one word. The milpa repeatedly exhibits a capacity to reappear in the most marginal spaces of El Salvador each rainy season. It does this despite multiple sociohistorical forces that have weighed against its existence. The milpa has a way of sticking around, cultivated by the people who return to and re-turn it. In Salvadoran Spanish, farmers sometimes use the verb *huatalear* to refer to returning to the physical space where the milpa was grown and will regrow in the coming rainy season. Like the milpa, huatalear is also a syncretic linguistic outcome of Spanish and the Nahuatl *ouatl*, which describes an area with crop residues and grasses that were burned and cultivated during the previous rainy season (Jansen 1998). The milpa is a space that is returned to and re-turned each year, with each iteration of the milpa being different from, but always informed by, the milpas preceding it.

Over centuries, the ongoingness of milpa farming has implicated a distinct set of nonhumans whose growth and movement are patterned by, and in contingent relations with, human practices. Very limited social science research has been conducted to date on the farming practices of Salvadoran *campesinos/as/xs* (peasants) who cultivate traditional three sisters varieties on milpas. The milpa is one of the small spaces in which everyday farmers often engage in everyday acts of agrobiodiversity conservation. Agrobiodiversity, which refers to the distribution of different crop varieties in human agriculture, is currently considered to be under threat or lacking any sort of formal protection. The United Nations' Intergovernmental Science-Policy Platform on Biodiversity and Ecosystem Services has declared that species and ecosystems biodiversity is declining faster than at any time in human history (IPBES 2019). This is also true in agriculture, where the rise of mono-crops in the Anthropocene replaces biodiverse crops (Hetherington 2020, 7; Shiva 2016, 7). Anxieties surrounding ecological decline call for top-down solutions to conservation that, while important, divert consciousness from everyday implementations of agrobiodiversity conservation. The Convention on Biological Diversity promotes targets including positive incentives applied to farmers supporting biodiversity in farmed landscapes, maintaining genetic diversity of cultivated plants, minimizing genetic erosion, and taking into account the needs of marginalized people (Secretariat of the Convention on Biological Diversity 2020). Forty percent of the global ecosystems' capacity to produce nature-based material for the consumption of humans is located in the Americas, which accounts for only 13% of the global human population (IPBES 2018). Seeds need to be retained to promote agrobiodiversity, but so much of the act of conservation is achieved through open pollination in everyday lifeways rather than in underfunded state-run institutions or demonstration projects marketed by nonprofit organizations. In-situ conservation refers to the open-pollination cultivation of traditional cultivars in their natural habitat—in this case, of seed varieties associated with the three sisters method of cultivating corn, beans, and squash on the Salvadoran milpa. On small milpas located throughout Chalatenango, in-situ conservation happens via intimate affective and material relations. In-situ conservation practices are imperfect and result in what are cross-"contaminated" seed varieties, those which may have been cross-fertilized with others due to the ways in which they are grown without physically distancing different varieties to avoid cross-pollination. We have little concern for the genetic purity of the corn grown by the Chalateco farmers who appear in this fieldwork, or whether the seeds they showed us meet quantitatively defined thresholds for heirloom criteria. Our focus on agrobiodiversity conservation in the Chalateco context is focused on what is still occurring in the folds of rural El Salvador, on milpas at the margins, on farmers' practices associated with reproducing a certain type of corn or beans in what may otherwise appear to be uncontrolled and unruly practices. What is important to highlight is that these everyday acts of agrobiodiversity conservation are fostered in the marginal folds of the global economy and are implemented in concert with subsistence lifeways that involve plants and the technologies used to grow them. Being cognizant of phenomena and theory in small spaces reveals the imaginative and agentive capacities of the people within them (Chao 2022, 7), particularly when those people are assembled with nonhumans that coproduce the phenomena of interest. The methods and concepts that emerge from ethnographic research on Salvadoran milpa farming are closely tied to the small spaces, farming practices, and more-than-human phenomena that we ethnographically documented in Chalatenango. These everyday acts of agrobiodiversity conservation are where we locate intimate entanglements that occur between humans and nonhumans, occurring and recurring with little to no interaction with national or international campaigns, demonstration projects, or funded programs. There is little academic discourse about these phenomena in El Salvador, but there is ample everyday discourse in the countryside about what, exactly, happens between humans and plants on milpas.

More-than-human intimacies are everyday sensitivities to, reflections upon, and attunements to nonhumans (Anastario et al. 2021a). In the context of this work, these intimacies arise from interactions between human farmers and the nonhuman plants, animals, and technological agents that assemble and reassemble annually in the reproduction of the milpa. Longing for, dreaming about, attuning to, and communicating with nonhumans are enacted examples of more-than-human intimacies on the milpa. More-than-human intimacies are implicated in farmers' motivations to return to the milpa and in their pride in cultivating heirloom seeds, and are testament to their unique expertise as artisans capable of growing a staple crop amid a global decline in agrobiodiversity. In this book, more-than-human intimacies are both the object of study and a guiding framework for understanding the material world with which the people who orbit milpas are entangled. Sometimes, a method is used (e.g., participant observation, questionnaires) to examine how more-than-human intimacies exist in a certain time and space. Other times, more-than-human intimacies become a lens from behind which we think up new concepts.

More-than-human intimacies arise in the more-than-human assemblages of farmers, plants, animals, and technologies that partially comprise rural El Salvador. Throughout this work, we use the category of *more-than-human* to refer to intimacies generated by the conjugation of plants and people. We also use the term *nonhumans* to specify actants within assemblages that are specifically and explicitly sources of action that are not human (Bennett 2010, viii). We interchangeably refer to people and humans, using the latter term to differentiate components within the more-than-human assemblage of milpa farming. We use the concept of the assemblage to avoid the simplifying notions of cooperation and conflict in referring to the ways that plants, people, and technologies come together in milpas, and to acknowledge the active role of nonhumans in bringing phenomena into existence (Guthman 2019; Tsing 2015; Bennett 2010, 23–24; Haraway 2016). Nonhuman actants may sometimes hurt the humans who intimately assemble with them, and humans repeatedly extract and devour much of the plant matter that is the focus of their nostalgia. To characterize more-than-human assemblages, we draw from Manuel DeLanda's (2006) conceptualization of assemblages as being irreducible and decomposable, composed of material and expressive components, with parameters of territorialization and code, and as having emergent properties. More-than-human intimacies are emergent properties that are brought into being nonhumans assembled with people. These intimacies "belong to the assemblage" (Stengers 2018, 105) of milpa farming, contributing to the ongoing entwinement of plants, people, soil, and technologies over time. We assume that plants are partly responsible for these intimacies, often communicating signals to the humans assembled with them (Chao 2022, 8). There are microgeographies and microecologies of more-than-human assemblages that could be explored beyond or within the parameters of this book (Pugliese 2020, 99), but we focus primarily on plants, agrichemicals, and the people assembled in Chalateco milpa farming.

Sometimes, intimacies that are generated between plants and people travel away from the milpa and through people who may or may not be in direct contact with the milpa. The movement of more-than-human intimacies away from the milpa through human networks occurs through "vicarious intimacy." Vicarious intimacy is both a process and type of more-than-human intimacy that arises in the more-than-human assemblages that are milpas. More-than-human intimacies are contagious and can be transmitted to data collectors who study them, artists who remember their family members' stories about milpas, and everyday eaters who eat with the people that cultivated the ingredients during the rainy season. As we will show throughout this book, vicarious intimacies can stoke in-situ conservation. When humans share intimacies born from the direct intimacy between human farmers and nonhuman actants (plants), we refer to this type of traveling intimacy as vicarious intimacy.

"Recuperative observation" is a method that we used to study more-than-human intimacies, and which is further elaborated in chapter 2. Recuperative observation is an adaptation of participant observation that partially reconstructs milpa farming from farmworkers' memories of past milpas. It is a methodological innovation inspired by Virginia Nazarea's (1998, 74) notion of "pockets of memories," which are "cognitive schemas regarding the evaluation, cultivation, and consumption of traditional crops." Recuperative observation involved recreating a milpa such that it elicited memories from other farmers who remembered seeing something similar to farming without herbicides, fertilizer, and insecticides at some point during their lifespans. Recuperative observation is responsive to the pesticide-related poisonings that have occurred over the last several decades in rural El Salvador and that haunt farmers' narratives of what has gone wrong with milpa farming today. Recuperative observation partially recuperates a past without claiming to restore it and is a methodological starting point for the ethnographic methods that unfolded from its practice.

The use of these terms may at first appear to be somewhat theoretical or too prone to developing categories that name something ineffable and "unobservable." The philosopher Isabelle Stengers reminds us that it might be worth using compromising words to discuss what happens in assemblages:

> The witches' ritual change—"She changes everything she touches, and everything she touches changes"—could surely be commented on in terms of assemblages because it resists the dismembering attribution of agency. Does change belong to the Goddess as "agent" or to the one who changes when touched? (Stengers 2018, 106–7)

In Western science, there are logical explanations for a participant observer to dream of corn fields after a day spent working in corn fields, but the occurrence of the dream might also fuel the observer's nascent fascination with corn, re-turning the observer's attention and fascination with the milpa.

Through reiterative acts of data collection and analysis, we have found that more-than-human intimacies are transmittable to those who study them through vicarious intimacy, and they leave their mark on humans who study them in unassuming ways. Marilyn Strathern writes that, in the ethnographic experience, events become interventions with varied and multiplicative subjectivities (2004a, 27), and that more data are generated than the researcher is aware of at the time of data collection (2004b). Intimacies emerge in more-than-human assemblages of milpa farming, affecting those who participate. In this book, we provide space and terminologies for thinking through the intimacies that form between the three sisters, the people who cultivate the three sisters, and the people entangled with Salvadorans who cultivate the three sisters.

This brings us to a final concept that is central to the data collection, analytic approach, and writing of this study. "Re-turning" includes both the concept of return (to the past, to the place, and to the past place), and the acts of interacting, reflecting upon, and generating. Karen Barad (2014) clarifies that re-turning does not refer to "returning as in reflecting on or going back to a past that was, but re-turning as in turning it over and over again—iteratively intra-acting, re-diffracting, diffracting anew." Re-turning is something that can be done to soil, cutting into it and piling it high in a concentric circle around a fledgling corn sprout that hasn't been given synthetic fertilizer at planting. Re-turning can be a way to engage in theoretical sampling (Conlon et al. 2020; Charmaz 2014), by revisiting "the field" to examine a theme detected in the act of analysis. Re-turning is a guiding action to think with while conducting analysis and writing. It allows thinkers and readers to occupy an alternative mindset amid the ever-quickening rhythms of Western scientific research. The ethnographic starting point for the data collection in this book began on the premise of re-turning that which was previously settled, subsequently ignored and subject to forgetting in research, discourse, and intrafamilial memories. We use the concept of re-turning to imperfectly think with more-than-human intimacies, and to reimagine the actants and people that coproduce them.

Chalatenango

Our elaboration of more-than-human intimacies is derived from ethnographic data collected in a town in Chalatenango, which is one of the four-

teen departments of El Salvador. Chalatenango is a rural department located in the north of El Salvador, sharing a border with Honduras, and can
be an inconvenient trek from the capital depending upon how one travels
there (Silber 2007). Motor vehicle rides give way to trekking on foot across
steep terrain, sometimes with the aid of a horse. In this region, economically
poor farmers have historically had more control over their land and more
freedom to develop their own paths than their counterparts in the larger
coffee-export zones of El Salvador that were dominated by fewer members
of the elite class (Todd 2010a). Chalateco peasants bore a disproportionate
level of violence during the Salvadoran Civil War (1979–92) in which the
Salvadoran state fought guerilla-leftist forces in a conflict that partially reflected an ongoing U.S.-dominated regional system (Menjívar and Rodríguez
2005). Many Chalateco peasants were displaced into refugee camps across
the Honduran border and later resettled. The conflict was so definitive for
the region that it has given rise to scholarship concerned with memories
and histories of flight, conflict, resistance, solidarity, repatriation, and postmemory in the region (Todd 2021a; Martínez Lara 2016; Hernández Rivas
2015; Chacón Serrano 2017; Chacón Serrano, Gómez, and Alas 2013; Alas
López 2021). In this same line of research, Mike Anastario (one of the co-
authors of this book) conducted earlier research on memories of migration
from this region (2019). He found ample agrarian memories imbricated with
memories of Salvadoran Civil War violence and migration, but which overlapped and preceded the time periods he was interested in. Like many oral
histories, there remained the analytic question of what to do with all those
agrarian memories woven into the "data" the researcher was not necessarily
interested in but that persistently arose and recurred in interviews about a
past he did not intend to observe. This book re-turns those memories and
gives them the attention they demanded through their presence, decenter-
ing civil war violence in the agrarian memories of Chalatecos who wanted
to recount something else for the outside observer who took copious notes
and audio recordings.

This current project departs from a practice of centering the Salvadoran
conflict and its legacy in Chalatenango. The specific zone where ethnographic data were collected will be given a pseudonym, as will some of the
people referred to in this book. This was done to anonymize farmers and
people in their networks who have been affected by what have been rapidly
changing political and social conditions in El Salvador. In this town, which

we will refer to with the fictional name "El Norteño," many remained neutral during the civil war conflict and did not seek refuge and repatriate like other nearby Chalateca communities. At the time that the ethnographic data for this book were collected (2017–20), some farmworkers talked about people who had to flee town and thus their milpa, losing their seeds in "la guerra de antes" (the war from before, referring to the Salvadoran Civil War from 1979 to 1992). They also recounted restrictions on everyday nonfarming activities "en esta guerra que estamos" (in this current war, or the gang war, referring also to conflicts with the Salvadoran state). What is notable about both wars, be it the one from before or the more recent one (which has continued to change even as this book goes to press), is the ongoingness of farming for those who kept on farming before, during, and after both conflicts. In some cases, active gang members could be found folding corn, pounding sorghum, and staring at the moon for signals. This act of farming the milpa is often overlooked or ignored, despite its centrality to the life-ways of people in a region historically affected by violence. The Salvadoran government classified over 99 percent of El Norteño's residents as "rural" in their census, and milpas are a salient aspect of the landscape. For the purposes of this book, the civil war conflict and the early twenty-first-century gang conflict is bracketed out to allow something else to come into focus: the affective processes and everyday intimacies that have been documented across ethnographic works among milpa farmers living in the region (Silber 2010, 2022; Anastario 2019).

Our focus on affective processes that arise in this region is informed by anthropologist Irina Carlotta Silber's (2010, 2022) more than two decades of ethnographic work that recounts a thick description of the affective logics of postwar intimacies and more-than-human instances of collective caring in Chalatenango. It is also inspired by the act of doing participant observation with milpa farmers in Chalatenango, where affective processes emerge and affect the participant observer in processes of vicarious intimacy. In many cases, the remote location allowed us to easily access multiple people with everyday experience conducting in-situ conservation of the three sisters on milpas. It also allowed us to participate in milpa farming. Throughout this book, we explore and re-turn those intimacies that emerged and continue to emerge through milpa farming in this particular place, despite the violence that often precedes social science research questions concerning Chalatenango.

Structure of the Book

This book comprises six chapters. Chapter 1 provides an archeological/historical overview of the Salvadoran milpa. Chapter 2 describes recuperative observation as a methodological starting point and provides context for methods and concepts presented in subsequent chapters. Chapter 3 is dedicated to more-than-human intimacies and presents quantitative data that assist with characterizing the distribution of these intimacies in El Norteño. Chapter 4 presents multiple methods for documenting and analyzing shifts in agrarian assemblages over time and focuses on the ways in which humans remember changes in agrichemical use. Chapters 5 and 6 follow milpa-derived intimacies into the realm of Salvadoran art (chapter 5) and gastronomy (chapter 6), using vicarious intimacy to understand and critically approach what happens as nonhumans from the Salvadoran milpa leave rural spaces and travel to more cosmopolitan and urban centers that render new modes of representation from them.

A Multiauthored and Multivocal Project

Throughout the chapters, we (the co-authors) use the term "we" to refer to three of us collectively. We have each lived in El Salvador for extended periods of time, and one of us (Elena Salamanca) is a Salvadoran national. The majority of the data were collected in the Spanish language (all three co-authors are fluent in Spanish), and Elena sometimes wrote sections of this book in Spanish that Mike and Elizabeth translated into English. Most of the quotes from people that appear in this work have been translated into English, but sometimes we present original transcript text derived from interviews with farmers in Spanish (followed by an English language translation of the excerpt) because farmers' ways of describing phenomena are particular to Spanish spoken in the Salvadoran countryside. We code-switch throughout the text, particularly when talking about traditional varieties, but we make terms accessible to readers by providing immediate translations for words and terms in Spanish. In chapters that draw upon ethnographic data collection, the word "I" is sometimes used to refer to the ethnographic data collector (Mike Anastario) in making reference to his field notes and/or experience. Other times, we refer to "the ethnographer" in the third person to focus on more methodological aspects of what is being presented. The work should be viewed, however, as a collective, multivocal product that reflects numerous thoughts, convergent lines of investigation, and multiple conversations between co-authors that occurred over relatively long periods of time. We have tried our best to produce a cohesive text that does not confuse readers but, rather, lends to its readability. Below, we each provide a brief narrative of our role in this current project.

Mike Anastario

I am drawn to the world of nonhumans. I enjoy raising plants and puppy dogs. I think often about the atoms shimmering inside what appear to be static objects. My predilections for the nonhuman are always temporary at best. When I begin to fixate on a plant, piece of art, or agrichemical, people quickly begin to orbit. They offer perspectives, offer new ways of thinking about things, and produce new questions that deepen my own fixations.

This book began as I was working on data collection for another book, titled *Parcels: Memories of Salvadoran Migration* (2019). In that book, I wrote about Salvadoran couriers who transmit parcels between Chalatenango and the United States, and their clients who send parcels. In rural Salvadorans' memories of international migration, so many narratives contained rich elements of an agrarian past. At first, I did not know what to do with all of this "data" and I let it accumulate. Milpa farmers recounted memories of the Green Revolution that were unfocused on my original research questions, illustrating their expertise and collective memories of cultivating the three sisters. These stories often derailed my research questions during data collection for *Parcels* and would eventually guide my collection of the ethnographic data presented on subsequent pages of this book. Throughout this book, we use the term "campesino" sparingly and instead refer to our interlocuters as "milpa farmers" to underscore their expertise and to evade the flat characterizations, tropes, and romantic images that, despite best intentions, typically accompany the word "campesino" in academic discourse.

My ethnographic data collection for this book was brought to an abrupt end in 2020 as I was doing archival research at the Museo Nacional de Antropología (National Museum of Anthropology) in San Salvador. In the early phases of the global COVID-19 pandemic, El Salvador was the country with the second-longest state-mandated home quarantine in the world (Fuentes 2020). Under the Régimen de Excepción (State of Exception or Derogation) implemented by President Nayib Bukele, my movement in the country and access to farmers was radically diminished. Despite the lockdown, milpa farmers continued to send me WhatsApp videos of fire they had set to their fields in the mountains of Chalatenango as they prepared their fields to sow corn, reminding me of the ongoingness of milpa farming. For a long time, this book project was unfinished, partial, and incoherent. I am lucky enough to be networked with Elena Salamanca and Elizabeth Hawkins, who codeveloped theories and co-authored this book through to its completion.

Elena Salamanca

As a historian, I have always been interested in integrating academic theory and methods with knowledge that was acquired during my childhood, knowledge that was passed down by my maternal grandmothers in the historically complex space of El Salvador. As a researcher, I pay close attention to personal experiences, evocations, resonances, memories, and even intuitions. These intimate experiences are not just personal, as they often lead to formal lines of investigation, like the ways in which methods were generated to study emergent concepts presented in this book.

As a Salvadoran historian, it seemed essential to me to re-turn the history of the Salvadoran milpa as part of the Salvadoran landscape. The milpa has often been neglected in Salvadoran history despite its perpetual presence. I am the daughter of a rancher and occasionally traveled to the birthplace of my maternal grandmothers, the Department of Sonsonate, and the city of Izalco, located under an imposing volcano. In my childhood, my perception of the natural landscape of El Salvador was that it was unchangeable and persistent. I stared at it from the car during road trips to the interior of the country. In political propaganda, the landscape was the idyllic setting for a future country that never materialized. In Central American historiographies, the landscape was often overlooked. The landscape appeared unusually unalterable despite environmental wear and tear, global warming, and, of course, the Salvadoran Civil War. By paying additional attention to the milpa that has appeared and reappeared at the margins of Salvadoran historiography, I was able to reconstruct a story of an agricultural practice central to rural and Indigenous Salvadorans (chapter 1). I also elaborated the way it was re-membered through the embroideries of displaced Salvadoran women, and eventually represented in various forms of contemporary Salvadoran art (chapter 5).

Thinking about my relationship with the landscape informs my contribution to the development of thinking on gastronomic extractivism in chapter 6, as it reflects my own personal experiences of intergenerational loss. I am an inheritor of lost consciousness. The traumas endured by the women in my family, from the 1932 massacre to the Salvadoran Civil War (1979–92), impacted me in profound ways. My great-grandmother was born in Dolores Izalco, the white part of Izalco, and never learned to speak Nahuatl. The parish records describe her and her family as "white" people living in a Castilian town that had strong cultural and commercial ties with Asunción Izalco, the "town of Indians." These colonial categories were still present in administrative and ecclesiastical documentation up until at least 1930. Despite being Catholic, my great-grandmother believed in *nahuales* (people who transform into animals) and in the *maldiojo* (*mal de ojo*, or "bad eyes"), and other forms of ancestral knowledge that some might consider superstitious. As a result, she did not pass on certain recipes to her daughter, granddaughters, or me, her first great-granddaughter. When I was just eleven months old, I became seriously ill, and despite being examined by multiple pediatricians, my illness was eventually attributed to maldiojo. This included a severe gastric infection accompanied by fever and dehydration, which can be fatal for babies. I survived the illness and subsequently became a girl with a *mirada fuerte* (strong gaze). Due to my mirada fuerte, I was excluded from culinary rituals and from contact with newborn babies because it was believed I could transmit the maldiojo to them. I was excluded from culinary rituals involving corn (such as making atoladas and tamaleadas) and from dishes that involved eggs or beaten egg batter, including the preparation of nougat (meringue) for cakes, *torrejas* at Easter, traditional *atol* (atole), tamales, and any dish that involved shaking the ingredients or using eggs, even for omelets. According to my great-grandmother, my mirada fuerte could curdle the food and spoil it. As a child, I was often taken out of the kitchen and even out of the house entirely as the women cooked in the kitchen, and I remember spending hours wandering alone in the garden while my grandmother and great-grandmother prepared food.

Although my personal story may seem anecdotal, it illustrates how fear can interfere with the intergenerational transmission of knowledge. Fear of knowing, fear of thinking, fear of speaking, and fear of doing have been present throughout history and have been inherited by my family. But as a doctoral student who studies and reflects on the past, I spend ample time practicing interspecies modalities of caring, which includes the care I provide to my family of two cats and the broader colony of feral cats at El Colegio de México in Mexico City. To date I have managed to give up twenty cats for adoption. Fear and pain have motivated me to re-turn that which has persisted but which has been pushed aside, and multispecies forms of caring are one way in which I have become intimately committed to the subject matter at hand.

Elizabeth Hawkins

Before moving to El Salvador, I spent nearly a decade as an immigration attorney in Seattle, representing many asylum seekers from Central America. The Salvadorans I spoke with expressed their fear of returning and described the terrifying risks they had taken to reach the U.S. border, but I also heard and sensed a deep longing for and connection to their homeland. I felt rootless in comparison, having been raised in a series of U.S. suburbs to which I had no family or other connection, and I was intrigued by the costs of mobility, the ways that my clients and I experienced our respective places in the world.

I connected with Mike Anastario soon after arriving in El Salvador for a two-year fellowship. When I read *Parcels*, I was struck by the way he articulated and explored many of the themes that had intrigued me, particularly the role of nostalgia in the immigrant experience and the way undocumented individuals and their families navigated their often decades-long separation. I could both relate to that nostalgia and feel my distance from it, because due to the privilege of having a U.S. passport, I cannot fathom a situation in which I would be prevented from traveling "home" as often as time and resources allow. When I heard Mike was working on a new book, I was excited to be invited to play a role in bringing his innovative research to a wider audience, as well as digging into the way milpas are portrayed in art and other domains.

In Seattle, my clients frequently brought me food items such as pupusas and tamales as gifts, and after I began traveling to El Salvador, they would almost inevitably ask me what I had eaten. Even after arriving in El Salvador, talking about food helped develop trust with people I spoke with: over lunch with a group of survivors of violence, they verified that I liked pupusas and that I knew to eat them with my hands rather than a knife and fork before beginning to share their stories with me.

I received a fellowship through the Institute of Current World Affairs, named for Richard Critchfield in honor of his writing on village life and the transformation of agrarian societies in the late twentieth century. The themes of my fellowship overlapped with different areas of Mike's research: I wrote about an annual corn festival ["In El Salvador, corn harvest brings together families split by migration" (October 28, 2019)]; a mother who relocated from the city to rural Chalatenango ["After city life becomes untenable, a Salvadoran mother moves to the countryside" (February 12, 2020)]; and about the ongoing significance of the martyrdom of Monsignor Óscar Romero ["Pandemic exposes divisions in El Salvador" (May 28, 2020)].

Although I moved to El Salvador temporarily for professional reasons, that move became permanent and more personal when I met my now husband, who was raised in a canton in Central El Salvador, and began raising our daughter. I witnessed her enjoying her first *elote* (corn on the cob), wondering if she would choke on the corncob, and learned about the maldiojo when her great-aunt ripped her out of my arms amid a great commotion after another cousin arrived after a long trip. These experiences inform the writing I contribute throughout this work.

Summary

In summary, this text is focused on more-than-human intimacies on the Salvadoran milpa in the space of Chalatenango and the research methods used to study them. It explores more-than-human intimacies not only as emergent properties of a more-than-human assemblage, but as a lens through to which to critically view and understand some aspects of agrarian lifeways in El Salvador. The descriptions and explorations are multivocal and partial, never providing a complete picture but elucidating aspects of more-than-human intimacies as they orbit and move away from the space of the Salvadoran milpa.

ONE
Milpas at the Margins over Time

En el jardín cavé la tierra y descubrí estructuras caprichosas con las que comencé una arqueología íntima.

In the garden I dug into the earth and I discovered capricious structures with which I began an intimate archeology.

—EFRAÍN CARAVANTES, "CASA," *JUEGOS FLORALES*

Synopsis

Chalateco milpas are peripheral spaces where the three sisters cultivation method is still practiced, where corn, beans, and squash are intercropped and grown into ingredients for pupusas, among other foods that produce the staples of the everyday diet in rural El Salvador. Chalatenango itself is a peripheral space, historically forgotten and contemporarily expulsive. This chapter revisits the long history of the Salvadoran milpa, drawing from the archaeological and historical records to tell its story of ongoingness in El Salvador. It provides context for understanding the current practice of Chalateco milpa farming in the marginal space of the country's northern highlands.

Milpas are terrestrial ecosystems made by humans each year, and milpa farming can be understood as a more-than-human assemblage. More-than-human assemblages account for the active role of nonhumans in bringing phenomena into being with the humans they are attached to (Guthman 2019; Tsing 2015; Bennet 2010, 23–24; Haraway 2016). The actants and people in this assemblage provide a basis for everyday activities, temporal rhythms, food, and art that contribute to the production of rural lifeways in Chalatenango. Landrace varieties of corn are selected and retained for growth after each harvest, persisting through human acts of in-situ conservation (similar to the ways in which milpa systems in Mexico have contributed to the genetic diversity of corn) (Wanderer 2020). Genetics get mixed up each year as varieties cross-pollinate and the milpa continues to be reproduced. Various actors, including agricultural extension agents who

FIGURE 1.1 Squash intercropped with corn on a milpa grown using fire and fallow methods in Chalatenango.

deploy modern agricultural science to the countryside, have recommenda-tions about how the milpa should, and should not, be reproduced. Milpa farming has a way of stubbornly retaining practices and patterns of the past while simultaneously showing an ability to assimilate to new practices and technologies.

FIGURE 1.2 Chilipuca bean vine latching onto a corn stalk.

The milpa could be decomposed into the corn, bean, and squash varieties that are referred to as the "three sisters." They grow well together, with beans fixing nitrogen into the soil, the corn stalk providing a growth structure for bean stalks (when they are adjacent), and squash providing ground cover to deter weed growth (Lentz and Ramírez-Sosa 2002; Lopez-Ridaura et al.

FIGURE 1.3 Parking lot attendant in San Salvador showing an ayote leaf growing on the side of a parking lot he manages, grown from Chalateco seeds given to him by the ethnographer.

2021; González 2001, 167–68). In terms of human nutrition, consuming corn and beans together provides essential amino acids (Lentz and Ramírez-Sosa 2002), and taken into account with other plants grown and animals hunted, the milpa farming system has shown an ability to meet general nutrient requirements for humans (Falkowski et al. 2019). There are many other actants beyond the three sisters that could be decomposed from the more-than-human assemblage of milpa farming. It is common to find sorghum, plantain, chiltepe (a type of hot pepper), cucumber, and other plant varieties grown for human and animal consumption. Snakes, *cotuzas* (agoutis), armadillos, racoons, and iguanas enter the space of milpas and, in so doing, risk becoming hunted by human farmers. There are trees, weeds, ants, rocks, mosquitoes, bags, handheld sickles, machetes, water jugs, food, and the people who physically bring the food and equipment in and out of the milpa, sometimes using a *mecapal* (tumpline) across the forehead or balancing giant bags of fertilizer on their shoulders. The moon, clouds, skyscapes, bird migration patterns, sunrises, sunsets, and morphological features of the plants provide signals to farmers about how to engage with the milpa at a given point in time. Farmers make decisions that are informed by years of direct observation and experimentation, and by the stories of other farmers about milpas of their past and their ancestors' pasts. The nonhumans and humans that comprise milpa farming remain in contingent relations with one another, with nonhuman signals generating human activity that re-patterns nonhumans within milpas.

The practice of milpa farming during the second decade of the twenty-first century is replete with materials that reflect the historical time period, including synthetic fertilizers, herbicides, insecticides, and fungicides, and portable stereo systems that blast the music of Bob Seger, The Guess Who, KC and the Sunshine Band, Madonna, and the Eagles into the soundscape as Chalateco farmers labor under the tremendous heat of the midday sun. There are the state extension agents who shape and codify multiple milpas with teachings about what should and should not happen in these spaces that Chalateco food comes from. Extension agents and community members alike sometimes scold farmers for using fire on their milpas, unintentionally enacting stigma upon farmers who already occupy what may be some of the most marginal, historically disadvantaged social positions in Salvadoran society. But the incursion of modern agricultural science by state extension agents is partial. One milpa farmer commented that when it comes to state extension agents,

pues siempre nos han dado algunos consejos ¡verdad! de repente los agarramos y si sentimos que nos va a favorecer y si no pues nos quedamos ahí con lo que nosotros decidimos, pero si siempre nos dan a veces buenas explicaciones.

well, they have always given us some advice, right! We'll use the advice if we feel that it is going to benefit us and if not, then we do what we decide, but they usually give us good explanations.

State extension agents may explain why it is not "good" to use fire to farm the milpa, but the practice of fire and fallow farming holds strong in the rural north. Small-scale farmers at the margins often do what they believe is best

FIGURE 1.4 Chalateco farmer with a *cuma* (sickle) in his hand uses a *mecapal* (tumpline) across his forehead to haul fresh beans.

despite and amid the hegemony of modern agricultural science (Nazarea 2005, 50). This is one of the ways that Chalateco farmers exhibit their independence and irreverence, not by defiant oppositional declarations but simply letting state representatives keep their dignity while ignoring information that is not useful to them (Graeber 2004, 63–64). There is the stigmatized use of fire by farmers, and the secret use of fire by farmers. The milpa is an assemblage that shifts but persists, decomposing and re-territorializing, from milli to milpa, in the physical space of what is today known as El Salvador.

This chapter serves to provide a brief overview of the history of the Salvadoran milpa through what Eben Kirksey (2015, 8) refers to as a "parallax effect"—a temporal rendering that rewinds the past and then fast-forwards back again, altering the viewer's perception as objects move against a distant backdrop. Because so much of the history of the milpa is located in oral history, we will pull in scraps of archeological, ethnographic, and historical data documented throughout the country of El Salvador. On a much larger timescale, milpa farming in the physical space of what is today the Salvadoran nation-state has been shifting, re-territorializing, encoding, and ongoing. This ongoingness is in part driven by more-than-human intimacies that emerge in milpa farming.

The milpa exists at the margins of a historical narrative centered on a type of export agriculture that radically reshaped the landscape during the colonial era, and which served as a backbone to the developing national economy (McReynolds 2002; Browning 1971; Williams 1986). Much like the milpas that reappear on the sides of roadways, between sidewalks, and on the edges of corporate parking lots in the capital of San Salvador, milpa farming has been both persistent and marginal across time. A useful metaphor for thinking about milpa farming over the longue durée is Donna Haraway's (2016) string figuring, which can be both "practice and process," allowing for "becoming-with each other in surprising relays." In this case, the relays concern humans, plants, soil, and fire that shift together over time in the space of what is today known as El Salvador.

Re-membering the Milpa over Time

Milpa farming in El Salvador dates back at least 3,700 years. For most of the life cycle of milpa farming, it has been an agroforestry practice that employs perennial, intercropping, and swidden (fire and fallow) cultivation techniques. The harvest has historically produced a staple diet supplemented by hunting, scavenging, and gathering practices (Ford and Nigh 2015). Much of what is today known about the pre-Hispanic, precolonial system of milpa agriculture in El Salvador is derived from archeological research, thanks in part to the volcanic eruptions that disrupted and preserved evidence of milpa farming.

Pyroclastic flows from volcanic eruptions have repeatedly covered and disrupted the land, and provided scientists with data to document a record of agricultural activities in El Salvador during the preclassical periods (Dull, Southon, and Sheets 2001; Dull 2007). The earth, ash, rocks, and volcanic material covering El Salvador's surface are materials that have preserved the earliest traces of Salvadoran milpas (Amaroli 1991; Sheets 1983). The pollen of *Zea mays* (corn) has been detected in strata of the earth in the Cuzcachapa basin of El Salvador, dated to over 3,500 years ago (Dull 2007). Archaeological studies show that in some areas, such as the Zapotitán Valley (today in the Department of La Libertad), agricultural activities were occurring 1,500 to 2,500 years ago (Sheets 1983). The domestication of maize in El Salvador is assumed to have occurred during this period (Sheets 1983; Amaroli 1991; Dull 2007).

Evidence of the intercropping of corn, beans, and squash (the three sisters method) in El Salvador has been dated back to the seventh century through the archeological site Joya de Cerén, located in San Juan Opico (Department of La Libertad), about two hours southwest of Chalatenango. The seventh-century eruption of the Laguna Caldera produced a thick layer of tephra (material produced by the volcanic eruption) that covered the nearby Mayan village, a small settlement founded near a river and surrounded by milpas. Its neighborhood was built with houses made of *bajareque* (mud and bamboo construction), and its inhabitants were dedicated to subsistence agriculture. At the site, there is evidence that corn (*Zea mays* of the *Nal-Tel/ Chapalote* variety), beans (*Phaseolus vulgaris* and *Phaseolus lunatus*), and squash (*Cucurbita moschata*) were cultivated (Sheets 2002; Amaroli and Dull 1998). Vines interplanted with mature corn plants were discovered at Joya de Cerén, and evidence suggests that they were bean plants (Sheets and Woodward 2002). The three sisters also appeared together in storage at the time of the eruption, over a millennium ago (Brown and Gerstle 2002), and the three sisters repeatedly reappear on Salvadoran milpas (and as ingredients in Salvadoran pupusas) today.

While pyroclastic flows disturbed and destroyed lifeways and milpas, they also preserved evidence of, and gave rise to, different ecologies over time. Fields of volcanic ash are grounds for agricultural initiatives and emergent ecological assemblages (Kirksey 2015, 214). In contrast, contact with Spanish settlers beginning in the early sixteenth century disproportionately disturbed local ecologies while simultaneously inflicting epistemicide (the killing of knowledge systems) (Grosfoguel 2013) and genocide upon the In-digenous people who were farming milpas. The rise of the Salvadoran Plan-tationocene (where food was grown in a system of multispecies forced labor) (Haraway, Tsing, and Mitman 2019) accompanied the rise in private prop-erty ownership and the development of agrarian economic elites from the sixteenth through nineteenth centuries. This social shift would push milpas to the margins of the developing economy, where they would nonetheless reappear each year, over centuries.

The sixteenth-century introduction of cattle by the conquistadors and Spanish *encomenderos* (foreign settlers with small land holdings) altered the agricultural landscape yet again. The use of fire in milpa farming depends on a complex system of land rotation and rest, with plants being tended to by hand and fire being systematically used. The grain-consuming, defe-cating, laboring cattle introduced by settlers allowed for the development of arable farmlands that could support a plow, making conditions ripe for the cultivation and expulsion of monocrops (Ford and Nigh 2015). Fire and fallow methods of milpa farming still existed, but a new form of Salvadoran agroecology was emerging. Settlers and Indigenous people could not survive by consuming the indigo, cotton, coffee, and sugarcane of the Salvadoran Plantationocene. "Pre-Hispanic" species of plants, sometimes referred to as "fruits of the land," were commercially exchanged between settlers and Indigenous farmers. In 1532, the bishop of Guatemala, Francisco Marro-quín, described seeing the following items in the areas that we currently recognize as western and central El Salvador: corn, beans, ayote seeds, chili, cocoa, cotton, pineapple, and melon seeds (Amaroli 1991). However, native crops such as cocoa, balsam, and indigo were in high and fluctuating de-mand between the sixteenth and eighteenth centuries, and shaped the rise of Spanish-dominated monocropping (Browning 1987, 124). While blocks of land were dedicated to monocultures, communal plots were dedicated to "other crops"—that is, much smaller portions and often identified as less fertile lands.

After achieving independence in 1821, El Salvador was one of the five states that formed the Central American Federation (1824–39) and became an independent nation in 1840. The founders of the Salvadoran nation knew that its greatest economic potential was in agriculture. The country did not have mineral deposits comparable to those in Honduras or Mexico. During this period, cocoa (native), bananas (introduced), and coffee (introduced) were central focal points for economic development in a largely agrarian population. From 1840 to 1871, tension grew over land use for subsistence agriculture versus market production (Lindo 2015). Land where monocrops were grown for export existed separately from communal lands used for subsistence agriculture (Browning 1987). In the late nineteenth century, a new legal framework had been established to distinguish private property. This new regime was built on the basis of the lands that the Indigenous peoples had inherited ancestrally, and who had been adapting to the new variations, laws, regulations, and reforms of the colonial regime until independence. In El Salvador, these lands were called *ejidos* (communal lands). Rafael Zaldívar, who served two terms as president of El Salvador from 1876 to 1884 and from 1884 to 1885, carried out the reforms to create this new land ownership regime based on privatization, which consisted of the plundering of communal lands that went to the state to be sold to entrepreneurs, especially those who were dedicated to the cultivation of coffee (Browning 1987).

By 1880, the first motion to abolish common land was introduced, where the Ministry of the Interior announced the conversion of the ejidos into private property (Vega Trejo et al. 2019; Browning 1987). This conversion was celebrated as a sign of progress, moving away from what was viewed under the settler regime as the conservative and inefficient use of land under subsistence agricultural practices (Browning 1987). In 1882, the ejido system of land tenure was abolished. Land became a resource to be exploited in the most efficient manner possible. The abolition also brought with it social control: the dispossessed people were going to be controlled and recruited to support the army, or to work on farms comprising what were previously communal landholdings. The former farmers became known as *colonos* (settlers), where a settler was considered a trespasser when occupying land that had previously belonged to a town but was at that time registered as the property of a person (Browning 1987). Most of the expropriated land was located in the western part of the country.

Subsistence plots in El Salvador continued to exist as the turn of the century neared. Between 1897 and 1899, the Swedish anthropologist Carl V. Hartman traveled to El Salvador and Costa Rica to conduct ethnographic research (Hartman 2001). In El Salvador he stayed in Nahuizalco, a Nahuapipil town in the western region of the country. His time spent with Nahuapipils, whom he referred to as the "Aztecs of El Salvador," resulted in some of the earliest data in the Western ethnographic record concerning the relationship between Indigenous Salvadoran people and their crops and practices, but also their feelings of disappointment, sadness, and frustration after the expropriation of the ejido lands. He observed how

> in the gorges of the valleys around Nahuizalco ... square and irregular plots extend, surrounded by fences formed by hedges of wild pineapples, plum trees from the tropics (*Spondias sp*) or thorny bushes (*Erythrina*). And among the groves of palm trees, orange and sapodilla trees, the houses of the indigenous people are scattered. Corn of various shapes and colors, different kinds of beans, bananas, sugar cane, cassava, pineapple, tomato, tobacco and a great variety of basic grains and other crops are planted in the fields. . . . Maize is the most important traditional crop. Before the land was parceled out, some thirty years ago, all the inhabitants of the village worked the field together and then it was offered to the god of corn. To do this, all the workers gathered with their tools and led by the elders of the community and the leaders, paraded through the field to the sound of bamboo flutes and drums. The women accompanied them carrying abundant food that they prepared in the open air and corn chicha. The same was repeated when it was harvest time. It seemed to be more of a party than drudgery, and everyone participated with equal interest in the harvest, which was communal property. The distribution of land in all these countries was, without exception, unfortunate for the indigenous people, who suddenly had to go from a communal system to an individualist one, giving the whites the opportunity to enter and convert the indigenous people into slave labor. (Hartman 2001)

While the ethnographic observations of Hartman are dated, they occurred prior to the twentieth-century genocide of Indigenous people in El Salvador, which contributed to the historical loss of traditional practices and knowledge systems. Re-turning Hartman's ethnographic observations provides some insight into the cosmopraxis of milpa farming as it was practiced prior to the early twentieth-century genocides in El Salvador. The worship of the water goddess, the sun, mother earth, mother moon, and plants prior to Spanish control have been orated in local history (Cosgrove 2010). The Popol Vuh (the creation narrative of people living in nearby lifeways prior to settler contact) tells many stories, one of which is the creation of the first humans from ground corn (Tedlock 1996). Hartman observed that when it was time to sow the milpa with corn seed,

> the Pipils hang garlands of multicolored Tradenscatia leaves . . . around their maize gods . . . small, crude stone idols . . . and at night they light candles and they offer them incense. I saw similar stone idols in the cornfields, a short distance from the Catholic church built in the 16th century on the altar of the city of Nahuizalco itself, as well as hidden in grottos in the river valleys. As soon as it rains and the gods have fulfilled their mission, they sink them deep into the river swamps and let them rest there until the next planting, when they come back for them. On the altar of the Catholic churches in the Pipil region, during planting, a clay pot with a shoot of green corn is placed. (2001)

The clay pot with a shoot of green corn could be reminiscent of the corn given by the twins in the Popol Vuh to represent a sign of their death and rebirth. But the shoot of green corn is also similar to the practices of current milpa farmers, like Chepe (see Introduction), who test out a batch of seeds to make sure they will sprout, experimenting with one or two seeds that grow tiny stalks from pots in their home gardens.

The Salvadoran economy was hit hard by the 1929 economic depression as coffee prices dropped and coffee farmers canceled the workers' already meager *jornal* (daily wage). Allied with the newly founded Salvadoran Communist Party, Indigenous people demanded the restitution of the ejido lands (expropriated between 1882 and 1886) and the payment of the jornal. On January 22, 1932, the army opened fire on the peasants and began a series of shootings that lasted for weeks. Many were shot in the coffee fields and milpas of western El Salvador, and Indigenous Salvadorans appeared to be indiscriminately targeted as suspected insurgents. Despite historical investigations, there are still no official figures on the massacre: the figures range between ten thousand and thirty thousand victims (Gould and Lauria-Santiago 2008). Surviving Indigenous Salvadorans stopped wearing traditional clothing, speaking their languages, and other practices that set them apart from *mestizos*, persons of mixed European and Indigenous ancestry (Tilley 2005).

Chalatenango was somewhat protected from these transformations by its geographical isolation, poverty, and neglect. Before the civil war, researchers

focused on coffee-producing western El Salvador and referred to Chalatenango and its neighboring departments as *tierra olvidada*, "the forgotten
land" (Todd 2010b, 16; Todd 2021b, 13; Browning 1971, 163; Pearce 1986, 45),
or "backward and on the periphery" (Todd 2010b, 16; Pérez Brignoli 1995,
247). Chalatenango was the least densely populated part of the country prior
to colonization. In 1855, the Department of Chalatenango was created and
was formed mostly from ladino migrants from other regions of the country
(Pearce 1986, 45). Chalateco farmers did not reap the economic benefits
of export agriculture, but they did experience relative independence from
the control of large-scale commercial agricultural production for export
(Todd 2010a, 20). However, the genocide of Indigenous Salvadorans, the
general assault on Indigeneity, and the accompanying erosion of spirituality
tied to farming would lay a foundation for the rapid uptake of agrichemical-
intensive farming throughout the country in the late twentieth century that
would repeatedly douse Chalateco soil with agrichemicals to reproduce the
milpas of modern El Salvador.

The Green Revolution and the Rise of Modern Agricultural Science

The Green Revolution of the 1960s and 1970s (the deployment of modern
agricultural technology to low-income countries) was effective at improving
yields and shifting reliance away from traditional knowledge and cultivars.
The proliferation of "improved" varieties and agrichemicals that accompanied the implementation of the Green Revolution sidelined traditional farming practices, and destroyed plants and herbs that once grew at the margins
of the milpa.

   Partial origins of the twentieth-century Green Revolution can be traced
to Mexico. With sponsorship from the Rockefeller Foundation, plant pathologist and breeder Norman Borlaug began conducting research on Mexican
wheat in 1944. Borlaug's improved varieties of wheat were more resistant to
pestilence, matured earlier, and produced higher yields. Borlaug's research
also led to the introduction of plants with shorter lengths that were less
likely to fall over in high winds (Phillips 2013). These technological developments would be deployed internationally during the implementation of the
Green Revolution, where selection, breeding, culling, and use of agrichemicals improved yields and shifted reliance away from traditional knowledge

and cultivars (Nazarea 1998). The increased yields were made possible by "transplant" varieties of wheat and rice that were fertilizer responsive, and that could lead to rapid changes in the food supplied to a nation (Borlaug et al. 1969).

While Borlaug focused on wheat, Edwin Wellhausen was a plant pathologist and geneticist who focused on corn with support from the Rockefeller Foundation. Wellhausen was the leader of the International Maize and Wheat Improvement Center in Mexico as well as the Mexican Agricultural Program (Rockefeller Foundation, n.d.; Hartigan 2017, 51). Wellhausen wrote about a corn with an alphanumeric name, SLP 40, that grew well with chemical fertilizers in the lowlands of Mexico and Central America, which was later promoted in El Salvador. SLP 40 was substituted by open-pollinated varieties jointly developed from the interhybridization of V-520 (Tuxpeño) with other varieties including the Cuban and Coastal Tropical Flints from the Caribbean region and the variety Eto developed in Medellín, Colombia. These "improved cultivars" available throughout Central America were a byproduct of the interhybridization of these 4–5 germplasm complexes (Wellhausen 1990). The improved seed was linked to an uptake in use of synthetic chemical fertilizers and "improved practices" (Wellhausen 1990). In its time, "improved practices" was part of a modernizing injunction associated with notions of greater yield and human welfare, but simultaneously contributed to the erosion and intergenerational forgetting of traditional practices in rural lifeways where these "improvements" were supposed to occur.

Borlaug and Wellhausen both focused on "improved" varieties and practices, with the idea of improvement being linked to yield. This was particularly important for parts of the world where poor yields could quickly lead to famine. Virginia Nazarea described how the Green Revolution tripled rice yields in Asia, simultaneously introducing rice varieties with alphanumeric names (Nazarea 2005, 76–77). The pattern was similar in El Salvador. Corn and bean production in El Salvador quadrupled from the mid-1950s and into the second decade of the twenty-first century (Orellana Guevara and Flores Romero 2019). Despite the ecological impacts of agrichemicals, these improvements in yield should not be underestimated, as they translated into plant-based foods that subsistence farmers with material restrictions could use to feed themselves and their children, and possibly sell for some cash income. At the same time, these "improvements" conflated notions of human and plant health (Hetherington 2020, 14) while denigrating traditional agrarian knowledge and reliance on traditional cultivars (Shiva 2016, 12). Borlaug et al. (1969) wrote that demonstration plots with "spectacular increases in yield destroy, in one stroke, the built-in conservatism or resistance to change that has been passed on from father to son for many generations in a system of traditional agriculture." These decreases in reliance on traditional knowledge and increases in the use of new technologies may have been guided by humanitarian aims, but they simultaneously promoted epistemicide and agrichemical reliance. For many farmers, the benefits in yield were obvious but "the so-called rationalization of agriculture was not that rational at all" (Stengers 2018, 93).

The deployment of modern agricultural science into rural lifeways may have been driven by people with good will, but it also produced epistemicide. Knowledge produced and generated in the West, namely in Western universities, has achieved a "superiority" in comparison to the knowledge produced by alternative cosmologies and epistemologies that are divergent with (and often subject to colonization processes by) the West. The universality of Western knowledge corresponds to an epistemic privilege that engenders epistemic inferiority among those outside of and unsubscribing to the Western knowledge production complex (Grosfoguel 2013). Western knowledge may be invoked and have the consequence of epistemicide—the killing of traditional (and often Indigenous) knowledge systems (Hall and Tandon 2017), even when it is being deployed for purposes with humanitarian aims (such as the Green Revolution). Like many forms of colonial and neocolonial violence, epistemicide targets children. Borlaug's focus on "the built-in conservatism" that was transmitted from "from father to son" would be met with efforts to inculcate rural youth with the teachings of modern agricultural science, eroding the collective memory of traditional agricultural practices by the end of the twentieth century.

Marilyn Strathern (2004b) writes that one way to think about the sociality of science is to consider "the kinds of communities created in the wake of knowledge as it travels in its diverse directions." The new farming knowledge of the Green Revolution was deployed in a multilevel manner such that its effects on farming practice were rapid and totalizing. Around the same time that Borlaug and Wellhausen were conducting their research in Mexico, the Salvadoran *Centro Nacional de Agronomía* (National Agronomy Center) was formed in 1942, which would in the twenty-first century be renamed the *Centro Nacional de Tecnología Agropecuaria y Forestal* (National Center of Farming and Forestry Technology [CENTA]) and would represent the government's agricultural extension efforts, deploying the lessons of modern agricultural science throughout the Salvadoran countryside (CENTA 2015). Beyond extension agents, the new knowledge that accompanied the Green Revolution was institutionalized through the development of new school programs in rural locations. One subsistence farmer who was interviewed in Chalatenango remembered how he and other farmers' children, who in 2019 were in their sixties and seventies, were brought as part of their formal education to local plots where instructors would use megaphones to show them particular varieties with alphanumeric names and provide instruction on how to fertilize them with ammonium sulphate. Even Chalateco farmers who today do not have contact with CENTA extension agents recall memories of their older family members being indoctrinated. For example, one milpa farmer who had never personally had contact with a CENTA extension agent in his lifetime described how

> mi abuelo sí, mi abuelo sí. El estaba "inscrito" porque él es de la generación pasada y supuestamente lo que me he dado cuenta de que esa fundación es de antes vea. Yo no, yo no la he tenido ni una vez . . . con el CENTA ninguna vez.

> my grandfather yes, my grandfather yes. He was "enrolled" because he is from the past generation and supposedly, what I have come to realize is that this foundation [CENTA] is from before. Not me, I haven't been exposed to it once . . . never with CENTA.

While these manners of deploying knowledge had an effect on milpa farming practices, much of the knowledge and practice of pre–Green Revolution milpa farming continued to stick around in oral history, and in swidden farming practices that continue to frustrate extension agents to this day. Today, extension agents, agronomists and agricultural warehouse salespeople provide farmers with instructions on how to use agrichemicals. Many farmers continue to be both interested and wary of what they have to say. In 2019, a seventy-nine-year-old Chalateco milpa farmer described how

> yo he hablado con agrónomos como yo me ha gustado platicar siempre ¡vea! Trabajaba por San Miguel y donde veníamos en el bus ahí venía

hablando con un agrónomo . . . y me dijo: "fíjese que nosotros en los estudios no nos enseña de la influencia de la luna; nosotros lo que si enseñan," me dijo, "es a cultivar bien la planta, sembrar y cultivarla bien."

I have always liked to speak with agronomists! Once I worked in San Miguel and on the bus ride home I was talking with an agronomist . . . and he told me: "look, in our studies they don't teach us about the influence of the moon; what they do teach," he said, "is how to cultivate the plant, sow and cultivate it well."

The observation is a curious one, because lunar cycles play such a central role for milpa farmers in knowing when to plant corn, in Chalatenango and in milpa farming outside of El Salvador (González 2001, 170–71). To everyday milpa farmers, the knowledge that comes from agronomists and state extension agents can be both useful and curiously full of holes. The agrichemicals deployed through these knowledge networks, agrichemicals that do make plants grow, will be further discussed in chapter 4.

Near the end of the twentieth century, another major impact on farming knowledge and milpa continuity occurred in the form of the Salvadoran Civil War (1979–92). After the brutal repression of the 1932 uprising, the Salvadoran elites and military continued to resist reforms and to brand those who supported measures that would reduce inequality as "Communist," including popular movements in the Catholic church that embraced liberation theology. To some degree, milpa farmers were able to maintain traditional farming practices during the war's displacements, largely in order to survive. Charles Clements, a doctor from the United States who accompanied insurgent communities, described how, as soon as the rains began in May, "everyone was out planting, from the individual *campesinos* to the elementary school classes and health collectives who each tended their own *hortiliza* (garden), as they called it." He went on to explain:

One morning in May, I came squishing and grunting up the eastern side of the "Grand Canyon" near Tenango to encounter an old man stooped in the rain with his planting stick, concentrating fully on the small holes he made and then sowed with three or four kernels of corn. I introduced myself, breaking his reverie. When he looked up and offered his name, Chepe, I could tell he was mostly Indian. After we exchanged pleasantries, I asked why he had seemed so absorbed in poking holes in the wet soil. Chepe answered that like his Pipil Indian ancestors he must stop and apologize to the earth each time he wounded it with his stick. (Clements 1984, 102)

After the massacres, the forced displacements and the depopulation of the cantons and villages resulted in the loss of landscapes previously used for the cultivation of milpas, along with the seed stores used to regrow milpas. This loss was not total, and it occurred in varying degrees throughout Chalatenango. Some Chalateco regions were heavily affected by war and displacement, and complicated by the Land Transfer Program in repopulated areas where milpas dominated (Todd 2021b, 146–48). In other areas, some residents were able to stay through the conflict. The ethnographic research for this book occurred in one of those towns that was not forced to collectively flee and repatriate, and heirloom seed stores were more readily available in these regions given that they were not as interrupted by wartime violence. Wartime nonetheless represented a second impact that is evident in the oral histories of milpa farmers today who can still narrate pre–Green Revolution memories of milpa farming in their oral histories.

While in the twenty-first century CENTA has established ex-situ conservation efforts through a government-funded germplasm bank, its resources are restrictive. During a 2018 visit to the germplasm banking facility, it had ninety different seed varieties on file for the country, twelve of which were from Chalatenango. Many of the names for traditional Chalateco corn varieties include colors or places: *Negrito* (black), *Criollo* (creole), *Raque* (a type of Honduran corn), *Capulin zona baja* (lower-zone capulin), *Santa Rosa con sintético* (Santa Rosa with synthetic corn), *Sunsupuleño, criollo amarillo* (yellow creole), *Tabero, Grano de Oro* (grain of gold), *Santa Rosa*, and *no lo sabe* (doesn't know) (CENTA 2010). The director of the bank described how approximately forty-five extension agents search for *semillas criollas* (creole seeds) throughout El Salvador, but the rules for reproducing the seeds (which begin to lose viability after about a year) have become barriers for success. Lighting, refrigeration, appropriate seed containers, and electricity were also scarce resources that affected the facility. The seeds were supposed to be stored at –20 degrees Celsius but were kept at 5 degrees Celsius. Seeds were stored in glass containers, plastic containers, and brown paper bags. There was no lighting inside the storage room, which was navigated with a flashlight that ran out of batteries while we were inside the room. The bank lacked the equipment to remove humidity from the seed storage room. In her research on Senegalese toxicology, Noémi Tousignant (2018, 47) writes that "the act of keeping is important . . . it speaks of struggles for and imaginations of extended tempos of scientific activity and of directed movement that reach for the advancement of knowledge and careers, the regulation of contaminated matter, and the protection of publics." Indeed, the director of the CENTA germplasm bank maintained a proliferative garden right outside the facility, and her intimate entanglements with traditional cultivars illustrated a lived commitment to conservation through action, despite the material conditions that weighed against her facility's ability to enact ex-situ conservation. The conditions of the nation's ex-situ conservation efforts underscore the need for research on in-situ conservation practices among everyday milpa farmers, particularly in Chalatenango, which is described in greater detail in chapters 2 and 3.

The Chalateca Milpa "Today"

The Chalateco site where ethnographic data were collected for this book is located in a tropical and subtropical coniferous forest biome of a central American pine-oak forests ecoregion (Olson et al. 2001). One study of woodland resurgence in El Salvador attributed forest resurgence to civil war activity, retraction of the agricultural frontier, and international migration and its associated remittances, with Chalatenango being one of the departments experiencing a relatively larger percentage area of forest resurgence between the early 1990s and the 2000s (Hecht and Saatchi 2007). But farmers still say that the mountain today is more "bald" than it was *antes* (before). In the case of storytellers who narrated farming practices of the past for this book (in the years 2018 and 2019), antes is usually considered the late 1950s / early 1960s. During that time, farmers cleared the pine-oak forest with fire, which produced an ash residue that fertilized the soil for two years before the land was allowed to rest and a new section of forest was cleared. Weeds were cleaned by *pura cuma* (pure sickle) before herbicides became widely available on the market. This was the time that some farmers remember learning how to farm from their grandparents and parents, who were born around the turn of the nineteenth century and who told them stories about what it was like to farm the milpa antes.

The stories that persist like those in the milpas of Chalatenango generate radical visuals of an ecosystem that no longer exists. The word *antes* becomes a refrain that is heard as farmworkers tell stories about the way milpa farming has changed and keeps changing. Chalateco farmers talk about how there is less shade cover for local animals and narrate stories regarding the disappearance of small streams and mountain ponds (Anastario et al. 2021b). Stories of disappeared microclimates and seed varieties that were grown differently before this present batch of alphanumeric seed varieties took root are told during everyday work breaks and evenings of rest. These stories are told in interstitial spaces, similar to the physical spaces in which Chalteco farmers plant traditional varieties alongside or at the margins of recommended varieties of corn and beans. Virginia Nazarea (2005, 78) recognizes how these acts of conservation and remembering "tell us that there is an ongoing challenge, a constant pushing back." These ways of farming a different landscape come from the time of antes, which happened in this space but that no longer exist. These nostalgic ways of teaching and relating are accompanied by ample everyday talk about precipitation, temperature, bird migrations, and the lunar cycle. Antes, it was not quite like this, but it gets the story listener to envision the time period in which we find ourselves today. In Chalatenango, it is not difficult to find milpa farmers who remember farming practices from the past, perhaps due to their remoteness, independence, or limited contact with extension agents. This is one of the reasons for centering ethnographic data collection for this work on Chalatenango—it is a place where the living memory of the rural past is readily accessible through farmers' oral histories and constructions of milpas as "sites of memory" (Nazarea 2005, 45). This salient attention to the milpas *de antes* (of before) foregrounds the methodological practice of recuperative observation that we describe in chapter 2.

In the Chalatenango of the second decade of the twenty-first century, it is difficult to locate imagined visuals of what it was like to farm antes. The cover of the book *After Stories: Transnational Intimacies of Postwar El Salvador* by Irina Carlota Silber (2022) includes a picture of a woman farming a milpa by pura cuma. The picture was taken by Silber's colleague and friend Ralph Sprenkels as he photo-documented acts of Salvadorans repatriating to Chalatenango. After experiencing a traumatizing flight to Honduras and spending time in refugee camps, many repatriated insurgents were left without their traditional seed stores and access to agrichemicals. The woman photographed on the cover is cleaning a milpa by pure sickle, backbreaking labor that yields the promise of corn, food, and return. While we do not know much about the woman photographed on the cover of Silber's book, what is notable is that she appears to know how to farm a milpa by hand, without herbicides, in what are most likely materially restrictive circumstances.

Many Chalateco subsistence farmers continue to exist at the margins of the formal education system and the reach of the Salvadoran state. Some may sustain a scolding for using fire on their farms, only to return to using fire as a clearing and fertilization strategy year after year after year. Chalateco subsistence farmers exhibit what Virginia Nazarea (2005, 50) describes as "irreverence, possibly more than resistance" to the hegemony of modern agriculture. Like the farmer quoted at the beginning of this chapter, many take or leave the knowledge imparted by extension agents. Chalateco milpa farmers keep farming the milpa despite wars, emigration, an influx of agrichemicals, the destruction of landscapes, and rural isolation. Chalateca farmers remember the milpas of the past as they engage in in-situ conservation while farming milpas of the present.

Conclusion

The practice of cultivating the three sisters together has persisted for thousands of years despite the numerous insults of volcanic eruptions, colonialism, genocide, and epistemicide over the centuries in El Salvador. The ways in which milpa farming has shifted but persisted exhibits a capacity for its ongoingness, with Chalateca milpas appearing year after year despite all that has weighed against them. This chapter was dedicated to documenting the persistence of milpa farming across time in the space of modern El Salvador. The next chapter re-turns the milpas de antes and elaborates a methodological practice of recuperative observation that directly engages with these orated memories from Chalatenango.

TWO
Recuperative Observation

Synopsis

This chapter describes the initial ethnographic methods that were used to study more-than-human intimacies on Chalateca milpas. It opens with an in-depth description of what we refer to as "recuperative observation," a methodological adaptation of participant observation that partially recuperates an aspect of the past and aims to foster more interactive participation from farmers during the research process. We use the example of an ethnographic study conducted by the ethnographer during the 2018 rainy season, and much of the chapter is written in the first person from his perspective as he recalls how he developed this methodological adaptation and put it into practice. Recuperative observation provides a methodological point of departure for understanding the intimacies implicated in milpa farming practices that shifted over time and are still recalled by living farmworkers today. Recuperative observation was also the methodological context in which vicarious intimacy presented itself. We conceptualize vicarious intimacy as a component of more-than-human intimacy that develops in the milpa and then travels away from it, through connections between people. This chapter describes the rationale and use of recuperative observation as a method that informed subsequent questionnaires and in-depth interviews that are elaborated upon in later chapters.

Recuperative Observation

Recuperative observation begins at a place of multiple endings. The end of one research project and the remembered end of milpas that were cultivated without the widespread use of agrichemicals. After conducting an ethnographic study on the ways in which parcels were entangled with affects in a transnational diaspora (Anastario 2019, chap. 3), I was affected by the nostalgia that accompanied their movement. As migrants awaited the arrival of food products made from plant-based ingredients, transported across transnational space, they shared experiences of longing, which accompanied their stories of food and the things that the food was made of *aquí y allá* (here and there). The ingredients of a pupusa (corn, beans, and squash), which began as objects in stories about the milpa and products that I accompanied across borders as a participant observer, could be more deeply understood by engaging in milpa farming practices that were used to reproduce the ingredients of the pupusa. By focusing this new phase of research on the cultivation of nonhumans inherent to farmers' narratives of the past, the research became concerned with more-than-human assemblages and their emergent properties. Understanding how assemblages shifted over time, coupled with my discomfort surrounding research methods available to me, led to my modification of participant observation with a practice of recuperative observation. I was able to practice recuperative observation due to the generosity of Chalateco milpa farmers and their willingness to collaborate and experiment.

Traditional subsistence farming practices in El Salvador have shifted rapidly over recent history and are poorly documented. Knowledge about them is transmitted primarily through collective memory. Virginia Nazarea describes how the traditional knowledge of subsistence farmers is retained in "pockets of memories." Nazarea (1998) defines pockets of memories as "more or less persistent cognitive schemas regarding the evaluation, cultivation, and consumption of traditional crops." Psychologically, the way a specific plant was cultivated and consumed at a given point in time references a "lifetime period" in the autobiographical memory of the farmer (Conway and Pleydell-Pearce 2000). Pockets of memories allude to ecosystems that once were but are no longer, and they continue to inform the practice of milpa farming and imaginaries of milpa farming in the diaspora.

The process of recuperative observation began within the folds of a memory pocket. A friend of mine, who I will refer to as Jorge, migrated from the

Salvadoran countryside to the United States. His undocumented journey was full of multiple failures and deportations from Mexico back to El Salvador. After multiple attempts to get into the United States, he finally crossed the border and met up with family in Colorado, emaciated from the journey. He saved his earnings working in construction jobs in the United States, and after accruing a substantial amount, he purchased farmland in Chalatenango. He made this purchase knowing that, as an undocumented migrant, he would not be able to visit the land until his permanent return to El Salvador, either voluntary or through deportation. Since its purchase, the land had sat unused, waiting for his return, intermittently monitored by his ageing *abuelo* (grandfather) who would sometimes plant a few *chilipuca* (traditional bean variety) seeds or monitor the growth of a banana tree on his grandson's land (abuelo was already in his early nineties when recuperative observation began). The purchase of this land could be understood as an act of restorative nostalgia by a migrant "with vision," who had left his homeland for better economic prospects in the United States with the goal of translating his earnings into a restoration of the remembered lifeways he had left behind (Anastario 2019, chap. 3). At the same time, his fixation on the land that he owned but could not cultivate, coupled with his generosity, gave rise to recuperative observation.

During one of my fieldwork visits in Colorado, we were both taking days of rest and I pulled out a sketch pad. I was experimenting with the potential of drawings to elicit memories, as visuals may aid recall (Anderson, Bjork, and Bjork 1994). I asked Jorge to draw an object of something that he longed for—of something that he missed from his rural past. I also produced a drawing of the *Pollo Campero* logo, remembering a time when I used to carry these boxes on airplanes with couriers. My drawing was of terrible quality. In my field notes, I had written that Jorge

> drew a picture of a milpa. Corn rows were lined up in front of mountains in his drawing, something drawn from a memory of a place that looked like what was put down on paper, more than ten years after his having left that place.

While I knew Jorge and where he was from, I could instantly see a Chalateco milpa in his drawing (figure 2.1). It was simultaneously abstract and specific.

The above description, derived from field notes taken during participant observation, represents a piece of ethnographic data. Re-turning those data,

FIGURE 2.1 Picture of milpa drawn by Jorge.

I decided to alter the method itself. I circled back to Jorge and asked if he would lend me the unused land to cultivate traditional corn for one rainy season. I wanted to cultivate his partial vision, the landscape he had remembered, because it also concerned land that he owned in a place where people still cultivated corn. This union of memory and place informed the way I thought about materializing a type of milpa built from memories of and within that place (figure 2.2). It is not just a methodological alteration but a privileged, artistic endeavor. I had the resources to do something like this without risking the consequences of what might result in a poor harvest. The land was "unused," and Jorge was happy to have activity there, so he agreed. In return, I would send him pictures, updates, and soil chemistry results about how the three sisters grew on his land that he remembered but had never seen in person since purchasing it. Even as this book goes to press, Jorge has still never visited the land he physically purchased in the town where he was born.

FIGURE 2.2 Picture of milpa created on Jorge's land.

Our shared experience, from drawing to cross-nationally collaborating on a farm, might partially reflect an "instinct toward placemaking" (Smith 2019, 199). In the art of placemaking, Smith (2019, 199) describes that a particular world must be pictured before building it with close connections (e.g., one's neighbors, family, friends, and/or colleagues), establishing boundaries that differentiate this new world from other familiar ones. I took Jorge's drawing and, with his permission, recreated an image of it on the farmland he had purchased with his remittances (but could not return to) in Chalatenango, El Salvador. His neighbors helped me produce it.

The recuperation of the original image was partial and imperfect, something in the material realm of El Salvador that emerged from the nostalgic gaze of a friend who had migrated but who could not yet return to his homeland. For the rainy season of 2018, I created a social media account (since hacked and shut down) that allowed Jorge to view the pictures that emerged from this endeavor. For a brief moment in our friendship, we were able to communicate intimately about something he remembered doing but could no longer do since he left El Salvador over ten years ago.

This activity, which felt more like an art project or a "performative experiment" (Kirksey 2015, 91), would also serve as the foundation of a social scientific strategy. In building a milpa that I did not need for feeding myself or others dependent upon me, I took this as an opportunity to cultivate some spaces within it through traditional methods that were remembered but almost eradicated from practice (e.g., clearing the milpa by pura cuma instead of using herbicides, just as farmers did prior to the introduction of herbicides). I aimed to grow some parts of the milpa without using any agrichemicals, something like how Salvadoran subsistence farmers remembered farming the milpa back in the 1950s but which was rare to see in contemporary milpa farming. This was an aspect of the partial recuperation of the past, never going back entirely, but peeling back a layer of development to engage in an activity (farming) in some ways similar to the ways it was practiced as the Green Revolution was just beginning. While there are certainly permaculture and other practices that have separate prescriptions for how to achieve plant growth without the use of agrichemicals, it was important to attempt to create the milpa in the space where Chalateca milpas were being grown, as roadways and larger swaths of terrain would not easily permit alternative solutions that I have personally used in home gardens (e.g., using fermented cow manure as fertilizer for corn). I also decided to only cultivate traditional seeds that usually appeared on the margins of Chalateca milpas. While I had heard so many stories about what it was like to cultivate traditional cultivars with traditional methods, it was difficult to imagine. With the Green Revolution squarely in the past, I had been bumping into the problem of the passage of time. In writing about stones, Hugh Raffles (2020) comments that "oral histories evaporate; myths and legends rear up, then fade from view. Only material remains, summoning archaeopoetics from archaeologists, just as it summons geopoetics from geologists, and poetic poetics from poets." By partially re-creating a milpa by using some techniques from the past in this space, I thought that recuperative observation would serve as a stimulus that might give me better context and access to a past that older farmers talked about and envisioned but which never materialized outside of intimate moments of storytelling.

Before taking this endeavor too seriously, it is worth briefly noting that the privilege required for a white male with a doctoral degree to enact recuperative observation in this space was salient, and I personally felt clownish doing this experiment. As I described to farmers in town what I was about to do, many commented that I was being ridiculous ("loco"). This was the whole point of agrichemicals—to make the task of farming easier. In thinking through other ways that I could seek utility from this endeavor, I decided to open up the space to experiments by farmers who helped me cultivate the land. I set out to find local farmworkers who could collaborate with me in the physically excruciating work of milpa farming without herbicides. This process, the act of designing the project and finding interested coexperimenters, was a slow, gradual, and nonlinear process spanning long periods of time. I wanted to work only with people who were accustomed, in 2018, to walking the space of a milpa, who could cultivate the terrain with guidance from their own childhood memories, and who would be interested in the project. I spoke with Chepe, who grew up in a farming family and whom I had interviewed dozens of times about his memories of the agrarian past. When Chepe understood what we were setting out to do, he recommended *los hermanos* (the brothers) who would farm in exchange for the local wage for farm labor. Los hermanos worked with their own family milpa, and the rest of their family also became involved in the project, including their mother who brought us delicious breakfasts of sweet coffee, tortillas, and *frijoles de seda* (silk beans) with *requesón* (a type of cheese) at the milpa about two or three hours into each morning's work. Roki, the family dog, accompanied us on each trip to the milpa.

The farmhands I hired, including los hermanos, eventually became my temporary coinvestigators. Not coinvestigators in the traditional sense (their names do not appear in this work, apart from an occasional pseudonym), but also in a very traditional sense. They donated their own family's seeds to the project and were able to take what they wanted from the harvest.

While subsistence farmers constantly experiment with strategies in their home gardens and on the sides of their milpas, scaling up experimentation is a risky endeavor for subsistence farmers who rely on the harvest to eat and feed families. Recuperative observation provided the space for a brief and fleeting moment of intervention into local farming practice that allowed for disastrous outcomes (like large sections of corn with poor yields), while also producing data and results that inform much of what is written about in this book. If farmers said they were interested to see what happened if they fertilized a particular variety of corn with a mixture of ash and chemicals at a given time, we delineated control and intervention plots and conducted the quasi-experiment. We observed unexpected outcomes of delayed fertilization sequences, and the farmers would engage in vigorous conversation about why something happened the way it did. In some of our plots, corn grew horizontally on the ground as opposed to vertically toward the sky. In others, the final corncob was so small that it could easily fit inside the palm of my hand. In *The Queer Art of Failure*, Jack/Judith Halberstam (2011) emphasizes that "while failure certainly comes accompanied by a host of negative affects, such as disappointment, disillusionment, and despair, it also provides the opportunity to use these negative affects to poke holes in the toxic positivity of contemporary life." Eliminating agrichemicals that were highly toxic often underscored farmers' attention to their dependence on them, provoking complex conversations about changes in farming practice and the ubiquity of agrichemicals, which will be discussed further in chapter 4. In this way, the milpa cultivated via recuperative observation produced moments in which farmers could see corn cultivation pushed to limits they may have never felt comfortable pushing on their own milpas due to the risky consequences of a bad harvest, and offered many moments for reflection. These were the primary ways in which the method was participatory.

When it comes to participatory methods, we academics sometimes have a tendency to flatter ourselves by offering "career advancing" co-authorship to people who are not constructing careers in academia. We may inflate the perceived weight of our actions in how we publish work that is likely to be read by a very small, niche audience (Graeber 2004, 71). While in some cases naming participants as co-authors makes sense (particularly in the context of participatory dissemination where participants may very well vie for academic career paths), co-authorship did not make sense in this context. The participatory aspects of the method, particularly the way in which knowledge was disseminated, included making space for moments and lessons to emerge that never reached a published page. Not all the experiments on the milpa were documented or written about. Microexperiments emerged and were brought to their rightful conclusions for those in attendance, who learned something and subsequently talked with others about it after the fact. Recuperative observation, for its brief life, recuperated some of the privacy of the field in that some of the experiments and learning would not be published. I tried to provide a small material space, albeit brief, for everyday ingenuity, experimentation, and knowledge to form at a larger scale. Failure was to be tolerated, even when rows and rows of corn did not appear to be growing as they "should," particularly when they were not subject to synthetic fertilization. Intervention conditions emerged, and we allowed for them to emerge in certain spaces and ways to see how this iteration of the milpa would progress given everything else that was going on.

Cultivating a milpa without herbicides to clear the land meant that as a sociologist, I spent a large amount of time on my hands and knees with a sickle, staring closely at dirt, weeds, and insects for weeks on end. This was not a romantic endeavor, and it was sometimes painful. It was physically taxing, and I spent much of my time "in the field" feeling overheated and mildly overwhelmed by insect bites. The sociologist Bruno Latour notes that for much of the discipline's history, sociologists have considered

> an object-less social world, even though in their daily routine they, like all of us, might be constantly puzzled by the constant companionship, the continuous intimacy, the inveterate contiguity, the passionate affairs, the convoluted attachments of primates with objects for the past one million years. (2005)

Staring so closely at the ground for an extended period of time helped me to consider and understand some of the questions that farmers ruminated on during off-milpa conversations. For example, the first time I accidentally hacked into a piece of soil that flew into my eyeball, I spent a good amount of time wondering about (and then speaking with farmers about) the chemicals that might be in that speck of soil in my eye. The composition of the soil, ways to move the soil relative to a stalk, the effect of various insects on plant growth, the discovery of pests, and techniques for clearing weeds with handheld sickles all became more than clear. Memories of older farmers regarding how difficult it was to farm without herbicides entered into and remained salient in my consciousness. The nonhuman elements of the milpa provided context for discussions and comments that were made while sitting in the shade of trees eating breakfast, drinking water, or snacking on guayaba fruit that fell plentifully from a tree in the center of the field during days of weed clearing and cultivation. Farmers did not blindly accept herbicides but used them out of physical necessity given the ways in which the cultivation of human-made terrestrial ecosystems had changed in recent history. Cultivating the milpa in this way made the context of the memories, especially the understated ones, more salient than my ethnographic imagination had allowed up until this point.

Practicing Recuperative Observation

After providing some context for how recuperative observation came to be, here I will delineate how I adapted the practice of participant observation to conduct recuperative observation and provide some examples of how recuperative observation was practiced. First, I tried to follow some guidelines:

1. Partially recreate a milpa based on local agrarian memory in which I would be a participant observer in the construction of the partially recreated milpa.
2. Pay close attention to nonhumans and ask for farmers to explain what was happening with nonhumans in this recreated environment.
3. Actively and repeatedly ask for guidance from those who are traditionally categorized as the observed (in this case, the hired farmhands).

To get a better sense of how these guidelines were implemented, I will start by talking about the act of notetaking. This illustrates some of the ways in which recuperative observation was and was not "participatory," and focused on nonhumans (plants). Participant observation has been the core method used in ethnographic research and has a long history in cultural anthropology. It was the core method used by Franz Boas during his time spent studying the Inuit of Baffin Island (Boas 1998, 16). In Boas' original notes from his 1883 journey, the text is rich with descriptions of nonhumans. In an entry describing an ice floe, Boas wrote,

The foot appears greenish; the deeper in the water the more intense the colour; by reflection this also makes the side surfaces of the floes appear green. The colour of the ice itself is generally sky blue. This appears only when one is looking at ice that is saturated in water, which makes it transparent enough to let in the light penetrating from above through the white upper surface. (1998, 56)

A few months after writing the above text, Boas (1998, 105) went on to write that "I have just been rereading everything I have written, to see that I have forgotten nothing." The nonhumans in Boas' notes can be read as a description of the landscape or perhaps as mnemonic aids, but it is obvious that Boas focused on and wrote detailed notes about nonhumans. In the social sciences, participant observation has shifted along with its practitioners' reflections regarding the gaze of the participant observer. Researchers have become reflective about the process, as well as acts of representation through writing. Ethnographers are now cognizant of "the tainted nature" of methods used in the social sciences, and the nonhuman elements evident in fieldwork and writing methods (Bubandt, Andersen, and Cypher 2022, 2, 10). As a quantitatively trained sociologist who had only later in his career gone on to spend a few years practicing participant observation, I personally had become transfixed with two aspects of the method: the act of observing is very much an intervention, and the act of encoding observations generates distances between the code and what has been "observed." A primary aspect of recuperative observation, in this context, was to recuperate "participation" without using predefined, and often over-celebrated, methods that simulate participatory aspects of academic research. I focused on nonhumans (seeds, soil, plant growth, agrichemicals, tools) and openly wrote about them in my notebook. I made visual maps and invited farmers to describe what we were seeing as I openly took notes about the nonhumans before us. The act of writing down what someone else is saying, particularly as farmers provided expert observations about nonhumans, re-shifted some power relations by reinforcing who holds the expertise. It also shifted the methodological focus to plants and their properties (Münster 2022, 141), and decentered the profundity of the ways that humans and their intentions participate in more-than-human assemblages (Bennett 2010, 37). While many farmers frequently deferred to my judgement (as an "educated" outsider who asked questions using formal Spanish and scientific terminology), this was one way to reiterate to farmers that I did not really know as much as they did about how to farm a milpa. This everyday way of traversing a field with a notebook reinforced a relationship of orator/notetaker, and reinforced what Helen Verran (2018, 127) describes as an "epistemic demeanor of participants as knowers," potentially breaking down some (but not all) of the epistemic barriers between informants and anthropologists (Gay y Blasco and de la Cruz Hernández 2012).

An ongoing focus of recuperative observation was to partially lose control of the intervention conditions. I still aimed to understand the conditions as they emerged, but I did not necessarily define their parameters. Intervention and control conditions would blossom and be openly discussed with the farmers who noticed and defined them. When fire was used, we would section off the scorched earth and start to do different things with it. Sometimes I would write down nothing but notes about plant growth in emergent "experimental" conditions that farmers had designed and were learning something about, for their own purposes. Bruno Latour's (2005, 159) assertion that "there is nothing more difficult to grasp than social ties. It's traceable only when it's being modified" became increasingly salient. Human memories of the agrarian past and more-than-human intimacies (my interests) came into clearer focus as we tried to get plants to grow using different and sometimes remembered techniques. Farmers' explanations of why plants grew the way they did included memories of what they had seen from milpas in their own pasts, and sometimes the techniques used to manipulate milpas included sensibilities that I was only starting to understand by engaging in the work of these experiments. As an observer, I was already modifying the field, but I was also learning from it. I chose to invest in, rather than eschew or apologize for, my acts of modification.

As the process of recuperative observation unfolded, my farm-working colleagues and I delineated five large "zones" on the growing milpa that had emerged:

1. A swidden plot (where organic waste was set on fire, leaving an ash residue on the topsoil) where no synthetic fertilizers would be added.
2. A swidden plot where synthetic fertilizers would be added.
3. A no-burn plot where no synthetic fertilizers would be added (the control plot).

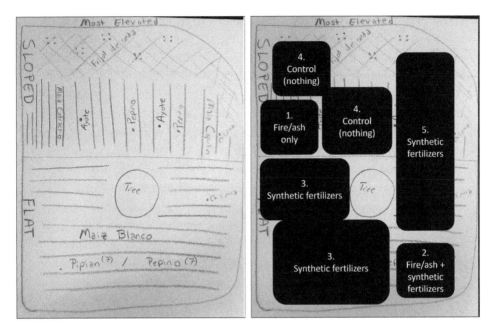

FIGURE 2.3 Maps drawn by ethnographer to keep track of emergent conditions on the milpa.

4. A no-burn plot where only synthetic fertilizers would be added.
5. Intervention 4 with a fifteen-day lag in standard fertilization.

The horizontal and vertical rows in figure 2.3 show where *maíz capulin* (capulin corn, see figure 2.5), maíz blanco (see figure 2.6), and *maíz catracho* (Honduran corn, also referred to as maíz raque or maíz hondureño rocumel) were planted. The sloped terrain alongside the milpa is where the frijoles de seda were planted. *Ayote* (squash) and *pepino* (cucumber) were intercropped in the corn rows, and chilipuca, a type of traditional bean, grew on trees located throughout the milpa. A guayaba tree was located in the center of the milpa. While the experimental conditions in the figure do not represent all the experiments that took place, they represent "the big ones" that usurped much of our collective time and energy. For example, while we repeatedly destroyed all the "weeds" surrounding the plants, every time the farmers encountered *dormilona* (mimosa pudica), a plant that folds inward when touched, we usually left it alone and sometimes called to a nearby farmer to come and look at it. Dormilona are not included on the map, but they were "weeds" that we selectively preserved because they were beautiful and cool.

The farmers could readily recognize the conditions illustrated in figure 2.3 without looking at the map that I regularly had to use, as the farmers were partially responsible for generating them and inherently understood the farming practices that demarcated the different zones. We did not plant stakes to demarcate conditions. We could identify the boundaries of each experiment by walking the milpa each morning. I would collect soil samples and bring them to the Salvadoran national extension agency for analysis, returning the results to both my farming colleagues and virtually to Jorge. The state's laboratory evaluated the soil for its texture, acidity, elemental content of P, K, Ca, Mg, Na, Cu, Fe, Mn, Zn, organic material content, and cation exchange capacity. Based on results, the state's laboratory also provided specific recommendations on fertilization (and timing) that were responsive to the analysis of soil samples. I had already conducted soil chemistry analyses at baseline (thirty-five days prior to sowing corn), and I collected follow-up samples at 105 days following corn being sowed in the ground (which corresponded to the period in which the stalks were folded), or 140 days following the baseline soil sample collection. The soil chemistry results were shared with farmers to determine what would be done and where, and the soil chemistry results were also shared with Jorge via social media communication channels (and an in-person visit to Colorado). This included fertilization recommendations provided by the CENTA soil laboratory, which became part of the experimental conditions on the milpa.

As soon as I had completed the act of recuperative observation, I found myself tethered to the spot where I began the process. I now had a better understanding of collective memories regarding the ways in which farming used to be practiced before the introduction of herbicides. It helped me attune to the way in which the current agrarian crisis exists in the landscape (Münster 2022, 141). I could understand what farmers were talking about when they remembered the immense height of the traditional corn varieties that were susceptible to high winds. When the grain cob has reached maturity, *la dobla del maíz* (folding the corn) refers to using the dull backside of the sickle to hit the node on the stalk below the ear such that the cob hangs upside down, which prevents moisture from entering the cob (during rain) and prevents grain rot. The practice is thought to have Indigenous/precolonial origins (Unión Rural de Productores de Cuautempan y Tetela

2021). While the alphanumeric varieties of corn typically "hang" from the plant after they are folded, the traditional varieties created a rigid triangular structure by the top of the plant hitting the ground (as opposed to hanging) while keeping the cob squarely off the soil and away from potential "pests," which was unlike the alphanumeric varieties that grew shorter and were more wind resistant. I saw the impossible-to-ignore correlation between applying ash to the topsoil and corn growth in zones where ash was present. I also saw older farmers shake their heads at my backward endeavors as they passed by the milpa, laughing at my avoidance of agrichemicals but also laughing as they stopped and remembered their childhoods. Many would provide pointed suggestions about specific herbicides I could purchase that would have made my life easier, almost scolding me to purchase highly toxic chemicals. I also gained a grounded understanding of the sequence of agrichemicals that appeared in the community relative to the Green Revolution, from the ammonium sulphate (fertilizer) of the late 1950s to the paraquat (herbicide) of the late twentieth century and the introduction of glyphosate (herbicide) in 2008. The partially recuperated milpa served as a visual primer for stories told by farmers about milpas they remembered, that once upon a time looked something like what they were seeing in front of their eyes. The stories gave way to narratives about how things had changed in this place over recent history. The narratives of agrichemicals that I obtained during this period were overlapping and consistent, making the endeavor intellectually fruitful despite the relative failure of our crops and abundance of uncontrolled experiments; much of our activity resulted in rows of malnourished corn that did not develop according to local standards of acceptability.

The act of recuperative observation drew my attention to experiences I probably would have never understood had I not physically engaged in the act of farming, such as what is entailed by growing a milpa without the help of herbicides. Cleaning the milpa pura cuma required kneeling before sprouting corn seeds and moving across hundreds of feet of farmland while hunched close to the ground. One focuses on individual stalks of corn and then refocuses on corn dozens and then hundreds of times. This involves removing weeds and building up a small mound of earth around the fledgling stalk (González 2001, 144). Cleaning the milpa in this particular manner is something that is remembered but rarely observed on large milpas grown with agrichemicals, arising only in interstitial spaces, such as the photograph on the cover of Silber's *After Stories* (2022) or Clements' (1984, 102) description in his wartime memoir. It is physically painful, especially on the back. Amid this pain, I also found myself kneeling before each corn plant on the milpa. Having bowed to the corn in the middle of a sprouting field, I might lean in on hands and knees to examine a fledgling leaf with my index finger. This act of kneeling, of bowing down to address the corn that will become food, is a humbling experience. Sometimes, when there was a potential "pest," I would find myself ear to ear with another farmer as we examined the leaf, focusing on the insect, talking about what was happening before deciding how to proceed. Kneeling before corn leads one to think about it, to talk with other farmers in ways that personify the plant, and to wonder about its development.

Kneeling before corn also speaks to an ethnographic practice of devoting attention to one nonhuman actant on the milpa such that it made my presence as an inquisitive outsider more acceptable. This is one of the ways I was exposed to the deeply complex postwar landscape of gang control just prior to Nayib Bukele coming to power. I was sometimes startled breathless to find a *marero* (gangster) standing only a few feet away from me as I worked. The marero would appear, an apparition in a field where one would otherwise expect to see someone arriving from a distance. On some days, I would be the only one farming in the milpa, and the marero would relax under the shade of the guayaba tree and watch me work. Donna Haraway (2016, 127) reminds us that the act of visiting can be "more than a little risky," and my presence in a homeland that was not my own reminded me of this risk on a near daily basis. At the same time, I never felt as though I were in danger, mostly because of how the other farmers responded to the presence of the gang member. At first, I did not realize he was a gang member, but assumed he was a friendly and curious local kid because of the kind interactions between him and the farmers. However, his presence was so persistent and reliable, I began to wonder. Unlike other visitors to the milpa, no one asked him, "What are you doing out here?" It was not until he asked me for a ride to the gas station and showed up wearing new clothes and a matching baseball hat worn sideways that I began to suspect his affiliation.

The marero, his boss, and I found ways of being there in that rural experiment together, of passing through time in a space that both pulled us in and pushed us away. Irina Carlota Silber (2022, 42–43) uses the concept of *violencia encifrada* (encrypted violence) to describe the way in which numbers about violence circulate and move out of El Salvador, taking on a life of their own as they codify violence for multiple audiences who digest news and statistics about Salvadoran violence. Researchers are just as subject to this codified violence, and it took me some time to let the category of the marero unravel as I began to see this individual (and people within his networks) in a more everyday light. A newspaper article never quite described the individual mareros I encountered in rural El Salvador, and I grew increasingly suspect of the sweeping generalizations that were readily applied to them. Multiple intimacies emerge through milpa farming, and the intimacies I developed with humans by focusing on corn, beans, and squash throughout that experience of recuperative observation most likely made my presence as an outsider with a pen, notepad, audio recorder, and camera more tolerable.

I end this initial description of recuperative observation with a brief story of the gang member who I mentioned. It comes after I made the realization that he worked for the local gang. He had already looked at my field notes and maps of the milpa and asked me to explain them. Perhaps out of boredom, maybe pity, but most likely kindness . . . he one day got up from underneath the shade of the guayaba tree and asked for my handheld sickle. He told me that he would work for a while and that I could go rest under the shade of the tree. It was a welcome intervention for a physically exhausted observer, although without the stamina of the practiced farmworkers, the marero lasted all of four minutes before having a smoke and disappearing back into the woods. This was not the first time that something like this would happen. There are easily digested narratives about who this marero is supposed to be, but as I saw him striking at the weeds under the burning sun without an audience or pay, I began to think of him as someone else, someone more complicated than an antisocial criminal or an orphaned kid for whom gang life seemed the only option. I later asked him to sit down and draw a picture of a plant from his past that he missed. He produced a psychedelic, unreal, imaginative picture of chilipuca seeds (figure 2.4). Planted by Jorge's grandfather, chilipuca seeds were growing on the milpa, and I was able to show him the aggressive vine growing on the trees in the milpa on a subsequent visit.

Years later, as I write up this chapter, I was told that the marero was taken to prison as part of the anti-gang state of emergency enacted in the spring of 2022. Nobody knows what prison he was taken to, where he currently is, or whether he is even alive. In this way, recuperative observation also led to the finding that intimacy could develop and be shared among the most unlikely

FIGURE 2.4 Chilipuca seeds growing on a plant (unrealistic) drawn by a gang member in El Salvador.

of actors on the milpa, producing new ways of relating that had little to do with predefined labels and much more to do with the nonhumans we inter-acted with, cultivated, and developed nostalgia for. Intimacy that formed with nonhuman actants could travel among and between the least likely of people we may ever want to think of as capable of bearing that intimacy, marking a complex experience of loss for that which has disappeared.

Recuperative Observation in a Sequence of Ethnographic Methods

Recuperative observation was one method that informed subsequent methods that were used to produce data for this book. Following the completion of the 2018 farming activity, I drew upon Virginia Nazarea's (1998) formative work on memory banking protocols to develop survey instruments and assessments that grew from this endeavor. I briefly describe the methods I used following recuperative observation here, which are the basis of much of the quantitative data presented in chapter 3. After completing recuperative observation, nine Salvadoran students from the Universidad Centroamericana José Simeón Cañas (UCA El Salvador) helped me administer a questionnaire to subsistence farmers living in the municipality. I used a chain-referral sampling strategy, which involves farmers providing "coupons" to other farmers that they would bring to the survey site. This sampling method assumes members of the target population know one another and are densely interconnected (Erickson 1979; Heckathorn 2002). When the farmers arrived at the site, they provided their verbal consent prior to completing a series of tasks with one of the student data collectors. The tasks involved the following assessments:

1. A questionnaire about farming practices and diverse seed varieties remembered from their childhood and used in the present.
2. Triads tests for corn varieties (asking farmers to identify the one variety of corn that was unlike the other two, and then to describe why the variety was distinct).
3. Diagramming exercises where farmers drew corn, bean, and/or squash seeds remembered and longed for from their pasts.

By the end of the activity, 128 farmworkers had completed questionnaires, triads tests, and drawings. Stacks of survey data and drawings regarding the remembered past and intimacies with plants abounded from this data collection endeavor. These overflowing stacks of data were then meticulously translated into numeric codes by the student data collectors, resulting in datasets that represented farmers and a variety of variables upon which data were collected.

One could certainly approach the numeric data we collected with hypothesis tests, but in this scenario my epistemological assumptions were not positivist in nature. The entire quantitative endeavor had been built on the back of something (recuperative observation) that appeared, in retrospect, to be more artistic than it was scientific. I did not have hypotheses, per se, but embodied intuitions about elements (human, nonhumans, and remembered aspects of the past) that now appeared in my field notes and quantitative data, entangled elements that in their encoded forms could be cut "together-apart" (Barad 2014). These data would form the basis of quantitative representations of more-than-human intimacy presented in chapter 3. While the above methods were used to characterize more-than-human intimacies on the Salvadoran milpa, there is a methodological aspect of more-than-human intimacies that I identified during recuperative observation that will be discussed throughout the book, but which should be briefly mentioned here.

Vicarious Intimacy

Vicarious intimacy is representative of the more-than-human intimacies that emerge on the Salvadoran milpa and then become shared between people, carrying the intimacies of the milpa away from the milpa through human networks. Recuperative observation and the methods that followed it reflected intimate engagements with nonhumans on the milpa. During farming, more-than-human intimacies arose and were shared between people who had contact with the plants. Farmers talked about what the plants wanted, how they looked, how beautiful they were, and how they were going to taste. Some farmers perceived that they could sense the plant and its desires in their dreams, or even remotely. After leaving the farm, a farmer might share a memory with me about the yellow flowers growing large on a squash vine running through the corn field, or the veins running through a chilipuca leaf. As I began to tune in to these nonhuman dynamics on the Salvadoran milpa, I realized that I had more points of interpersonal connection with farmers who were also attuned to botanical phenomena. It was like sharing an appreciation for ineffable aspects of art with artists, except in this case the ineffable aspects of what was being shared were being shared with other farmers (often between men). The shared intimacy reinforced my interest in plants on the milpa. This was my own experience of vicarious intimacy, which refers to the intimacy that travels between humans connected to farmers for whom more-than-human intimacies emerged.

Vicarious intimacy is contagious and capable of moving between all sorts of people who connect with those who tend the milpa. It also emerged within the student research team as they collected survey data from farmworkers. After one particularly long day of data collection, a Salvadoran student from the capital told me that he was interested in growing chilipuca. He had never grown beans before, but he had developed an interest in growing chilipuca as a result of repeatedly interviewing farmers who spoke affectionately about growing chilipuca. Similar to the development of "vicarious trauma" or "secondary trauma" that can occur in data collectors when conducting interviews with individuals who have had traumatic or adverse life experiences, vicarious intimacy was intimacy transmitted to and experienced by the interviewer.

The survey data collection team manager, Miguel Arias, was a student at UCA El Salvador during the data collection endeavor. Two years after the data collection experience had ended, Miguel sat down with me at a café in San Salvador and explained how

> not just an interest in plants arose from this, but also an interest in these peoples' lives. I feel like it also helped me to gain empathy. . . . I was never as close as I was after the experience. . . . Farmers were always in this outside world for me . . . after that I got closer. I was in their place, I was asking about their lives . . . it became much more intimate for me. I started gaining certain knowledge. . . . I also got a job out of that. I worked in Chalatenango . . . I developed this interest. It's still growing. It's something that was planted like a seed. It grew a connection that I didn't have before. I was introduced to an entirely new world. I became interested in biodiversity. We asked if there were certain species of crops that they used to plant when they were children. And some of them remembered certain species that don't exist anymore . . . I didn't know that H5 corn introduced by the government killed off a lot of the varieties that people used to keep. I also understood that these bonds between food and people were broken. Now I recognize campesinos as professors in growing crops.

The more-than-human intimacy that grew between farmers and nonhuman actants on the milpa had a way of being preserved and sometimes traveling

FIGURE 2.5   Maíz capulin and maíz blanco.

away from the milpa. When farmers talk to nonfarmers about their intimacy with plants in such a way as to infect the data collector with an interest in traditional corn and bean varieties, this, too, is vicarious intimacy.

Vicarious intimacy reflected both a conceptual finding and a limitation of recuperative observation that I only realized in retrospect. The key in-

FIGURE 2.5 Maíz capulin.

formants who I was most closely tied to, and who I interacted with on a daily basis, were mostly men. While our survey (described in greater detail in chapter 3) included farmers who identified as women (16% of the final analytic sample), the observational data were heavily focused on men. But beyond acknowledging that women do farm the milpa, it is important to underscore that women also participate in labor associated with feeding milpa farmers, both on the milpa as farmers tend the land and in processing the harvest. Producing food from the three sisters harvested from milpas is another area where women actively and regularly participate in processes of vicarious intimacy concerning the milpa. In writing about paradoxes at the core of agriculture in India, Hayden Kantor (2020) describes a generation of older men who had farmed the local land for their entire lives, relied on day laborers and sharecroppers for support, and planned to pass on property to sons but felt reluctant about them following in their footsteps. Kantor (2019) also highlights "the labor of sensing that undergirds productive labor" in generating foods that sustain the body. The labor of sensing tastes and smells of traditional varieties that become food re-attune farmers' attention back to these qualities of the plants they grow (this will be described further in chapter 3). Women responsible for processing the harvest into food inculcate preferences through cooking that are made salient during plant growth processes on milpas. Vicarious intimacy is one of the many ways in which we may later understand how conservation efforts and food bring us back to the Salvadoran milpa, and the traditional varieties therein, at a time when so much seems to be subject to loss.

Conclusion

This chapter began with a description of recuperative observation, an adaptation of participant observation that was built from farmworkers' memories, and which partially recuperated a past without claiming to restore it. Recuperative observation leveraged a way to manipulate a human-made terrestrial ecosystem such that it elicited memories from other farmers who remembered seeing something similar to what materialized at some point during their lifespans. It was an ethnographic method that assisted with the rearticulation of subordinated sensibilities, helping to reveal other worlds that existed within modernity (Law and Lien 2018, 158). Recuperative observation provided rich context that informed the implementation of subsequent methods that were used to study more-than-human intimacies among farmers, helping us to refine life history elicitation methods used in biodiversity memory banking methods that will be presented in chapter 3. Finally, recuperative observation provided the context in which vicarious intimacy could emerge, be explored, and inform the way we understand more-than-human intimacies on the Salvadoran milpa. As a concept and methodological intervention, recuperative observation could potentially be adapted and stimulate new ways of thinking about recuperating other things that seem "lost" in Chalatenango, such as land that no longer yields as it should, or recuperating intimacies in a postwar environment where reconciliation is fraught. We will continue to explore the theme of vicarious intimacy as it travels through the contexts explored in this book, making its way into art, consumption, and the diaspora, and the ways it returns our attention back to the Salvadoran milpa.

THREE
More-than-Human Intimacies

Synopsis

In this chapter, we define and characterize *more-than-human intimacies*, a concept we use to refer to Chalateco farmers' everyday attunements to, sensitivities regarding, and affectively charged experiences of nonhumans (in the case of this chapter, seed and plant varieties). More-than-human intimacies foster the in-situ conservation of traditional cultivars. The intimacies explored in this chapter are material and expressive, being "more-than" human because they involve a sense of human intimacy that is conjugated with botanical actants. Nostalgia for cultivars of the past, dreaming about the milpa, and sensations of attachment to the harvest are some forms of more-than-human intimacies that are described. We illustrate aspects of more-than-human intimacies with a variety of research methods, including field notes, questionnaires, triads tests, and drawings. Part of the analysis is focused on a quantitative analysis of self-reported intimacies and is subject to a machine learning algorithm that elucidates ethnographic bias in this study of intimacy. We conclude with a more concise, but nonetheless working concept of more-than-human intimacies applied to the context of Chalateca milpa farming.

Gerardo

Gerardo has a milpa surrounding his home in El Norteño. Gerardo and I (Mike, the ethnographer) met after a student data collector administered a questionnaire to him regarding his agricultural practices, memories, and experiences of more-than-human intimacy. Gerardo had come back to the data collection site where the students were administering the surveys and expressed that he would like to take the survey again. I spent the earlier part of my career studying violence and trauma, and during that time I never encountered a scenario where a participant wanted to repeat the study procedure. There was a small financial incentive associated with completing the questionnaire, but Gerardo expressed that he did not care about the financial incentive. He just wanted to be interviewed again because he enjoyed the experience.

No sooner had I begun speaking with Gerardo about his curious desire to be interviewed twice when Gerardo took some chilipuca seeds out of his pocket and placed them in my hand. I had never seen seeds quite like these. Chilipuca seeds are traditional legume varieties that appear in all sorts of shapes and sizes. The vine grows aggressively, winding around trees and producing leaves with distinct veins branching out from the petiole (see figures 3.1, 3.2, and 3.3).

One of the chilipuca seeds was larger than the other, and Gerardo explained that they were distinct varieties. He added that both seeds were from lineages blessed by Óscar Romero in 1979 just before he was executed. Gerardo described how the larger seed was *chilipuca chispota* and how the smaller seed was *chilipuca de seda* (silk chilipuca).

I asked Gerardo if he wanted to participate in a different type of interview (a semistructured interview that I was conducting with a smaller group of farmers). Gerardo agreed to be audio-recorded. Gerardo had a poetic way of speaking about his milpa, and we illustrate his utterances in Spanish (followed by an English translation) to transmit to readers a sense of how he spoke about his milpa.

> Usted puede ir en la tarde o de mañana y usted ve, si usted ha sembrado bien, ha cultivado bien su milpa . . . ve un solo mar como que este viendo el agua, como que este viendo un lago . . . de una parte se ve de un modo y de otra parte, si usted la ve de abajo, o de arriba para abajo se ve un solo corte de maíz, no se ve tierra solo maíz.

> You can go to the milpa in the afternoon or in the morning and you see, if you have done a good job planting everything, that you have

FIGURE 3.1 A chilipuca leaf.

cultivated your cornfield well . . . you just see a sea as if you were looking at the water, as if you were looking at a lake . . . on one side it looks one way and on the other side, if you look at it from below, or from above looking below you can see a single cut of corn, you can't see land, just corn.

FIGURE 3.2 Two chilipuca seeds in an opened pod.

Gerardo's description evoked the words of the Salvadoran poet Alfredo Espino (1996), who recounted how *eran mares los cañales que yo contemplaba un día* ("the sugarcane fields were seas that I contemplated one day"). Gerardo contemplated looking at the corn as though one were looking at the water, observing multitudes of plants all at once. His description of the

FIGURE 3.3 Chilipuca seeds on a tarp.

different perspectives with which he gazed upon the milpa reminded me of a dream I had about corn fields, and the way I learned to stare out over the corn rows as though trying to see a pattern in an autostereogram (to visually see the bees carrying pollen between plants, or the presence of insects that may signal the start of a plague). Gerardo described how he could remotely sense other beings that were present in the milpa, even if he was not there.

A una distancia . . . si usted va por la milpa mía y yo estoy arriba yo siento que anda alguien en la milpa . . . me muevo usted lo siente o si pasa un animal siente, debajo del maíz que pase se siente.

From a distance . . . if you go through my cornfield and I'm up there (away from home), I feel when someone is walking in the cornfield . . . if I move, you feel it or if an animal passes through it you feel it, if it passes underneath the corn you feel it.

Gerardo was describing senses, far more attuned than my own, that sometimes seem to grow among those who work reiteratively with large quantities of corn and bean varieties over the plants' growth cycles. After conducting a round of recuperative observation, I was vaguely familiar with this sensation. The physical reach of Gerardo's sensorium at any one given moment in time might sound superhuman, or perhaps unreal, but we prefer to characterize these renderings of intimacy with the milpa as more-than-human. Gerardo perceived that he could feel what was happening in a corn field even when he was not near it, and when he was near it, he visually observed it through various angles and perspectives.

Gerardo also dreamed of corn. As he describes it,

Sueño. Sueño como a veces uno le pone amor a las cosas, a los trabajos, como tiene su cultivo, siente una alegría y está pensando cómo va a ser, como quiere Dios que sea. Si va a ser buena, va a producir . . . yo ya he visto en sueños, he visto que veo el maíz grande con mazorcas grandes y he visto también el frijolar que está todo bueno. Yo me lo imagino desde que voy sembrando que pongo una chilipuca . . . me lo estoy imaginando yo como será en mi imaginación, como ya los he visto, será así de alta y cargadito hasta abajo . . . solo me imagino, a veces he soñado.

I dream. Sometimes I dream about how one puts love to things, to work, how you have your farm, you feel joy thinking about how it is going to be, how God wants it to be. If it is going to be good, if it will be productive, I have seen this in dreams, I have seen large corn with large ears and I have also seen that all is well with the bean field. I imagine it from the moment I sow a chilipuca seed, I am imagining how it will be in my imagination, as I have already seen it, it will be this high and loaded [with beans throughout the vine], I only imagine, sometimes I have dreamed it.

The temporal interplay in Gerardo's narrative, his willful prospection, and actual dreams attune him to the plants and help explain what might otherwise appear to be his obsessive attention to his milpa. Gerardo's dreams bear similarities to the oneiric perspectivism involving "an altered and alternating state of consciousness" described by Sophie Chao (2022, 190) in her examination of multispecies entanglements of oil palm plantations in West Papua. Chao (2022, 195) finds collective experiences of dreams as a way for interspecies relations to be articulated and for humans to reckon interhuman relations.

Receiving his watchful care, Gerardo cultivates *maíz criollo amarillo* (yellow creole corn), maíz blanco, and chilipuca varieties each year. Gerardo's seeds were grown like this by his father since before Gerardo remembers the seeds being blessed by Óscar Romero, forty years before the date

FIGURE 3.4 Mural depicting seeds being blessed by Óscar Romero. Mural by Patricia Deras and Verónica Deras.

of the recorded interview. This is a detail linked to Gerardo's memory of the seeds that comes alive as Gerardo gifts and talks about his seeds with others.

Gerardo gave numerous seed varieties to me. Gerardo invited me to the milpa surrounding his house, which at first appeared to look something like a garden, but with chilipuca chispota vines climbing aggressively high into the mango trees. Gerardo shared traditional corn and bean seeds with me and asked that I share them with others. Eventually, some students and colleagues would go on to ask me for the chilipuca seeds or express an interest in how to grow them, even if they had never grown nor tasted chilipuca. I exchanged chilipuca seeds with other farmers who did unexpected favors or who simply asked for them. As the seeds moved between hands of farmers who talked about the varieties and how they grow, a vicarious intimacy emerged between people as their attention was drawn back to the milpa. Long after the interview, the conversations I had with people who are not farmers but who developed an interest in the chilipuca seeds that I repeatedly found in and throughout my belongings, in El Salvador and the United States, inevitably led back to Gerardo and the memories of the seeds he transmitted by gifting them to me.

Codifying Intimacy

Intimacy is something that is difficult to study, and it is something that entangles ethnographers with people as they study it. In her ethnographic account of the one and one-half insurgent generation from Chalatenango, the anthropologist Irina Carlota Silber (2022) refers to her methodology as being "based on a protracted and intimate arc that attends to shifts in solidarity." Intimacies develop between researchers and people, plants, and objects. Intimacies entangle the researcher with the field of study, sometimes making it difficult to see or to isolate those intimacies due to their ubiquity and the ways in which intimacies are managed. The study of intimacies can lead to inductive biases, but the process of studying them can also unfold like a fractal, leading to depth and the development of new concepts as one delves deeper into the intimacies with which one becomes entangled.

Representing intimacy with numbers and statistics is one way of studying intimacy that almost seems to stand in contradistinction to an ethnographic study of intimacy. But understanding patterns in self-reported experiences of intimacy can lead to insights regarding distributions of intimacy. In the context of this study, more-than-human intimacies are reinforced through acts of dreaming about, longing for, and imagining nonhumans in the absence of physical contact. More-than-human intimacies travel away from the milpa between humans through vicarious intimacy. As we begin to attempt to codify intimacy and represent it with numbers, the act of codification should not be taken too seriously. Rather, the purpose is to get a sense of the ways in which more-than-human intimacy may be patterned. We understand that many of us who study intimacy detect it through the use of qualitative methods and the use of an inductive approach that leads to thick descriptions and the genesis or articulation of concepts. Using quantitative methods to understand intimacy feels almost alien, nonhuman, or perhaps more-than-human. However, many who practice participant observation now use computers and software packages to type up field notes, transcribe interviews, and code the text. Computers have become an integral part of writing, publishing, and representing. Why not consider other capabilities of machines to aid in understanding patterns that may be inherent to collected data regarding intimacy?

Below, we begin with a description of more-than-human intimacies as they occurred and were first experienced by the ethnographer in the context of field notes. Then, we explore other methods used to characterize some of the distribution of more-than-human intimacies among milpa farmers in El Norteño. As we explore some of the variables that more-than-human intimacies are entangled with, we invite the reader to try to discern patterns. Machines have a way of presenting patterns in data back to us, sometimes in ways that might have been difficult to see as an embodied observer. We are inspired by Gerardo, who described looking out at a sea of corn, finding different perspectives for viewing something that he knew so well. He looked at the corn fields as though he were staring at the sea. We are looking at patterns of more-than-human intimacies through code.

More-than-Human Intimacies Encoded in Field Notes

Field notes from the first time the ethnographer began engaging in corn-farming tasks as a participant observer provide data on more-than-human intimacies. After his first day doing participant observation on a milpa in 2017, he wrote the following entry into his notes:

> I am so tired. I am headachy . . . I have a rash between my legs, and I can't get my temperature down. I'm tired and itchy and headachy. When I took a nap, I dreamed of corn. By 4:30 p.m., I was still unable to do anything. I had a bad headache and muscle cramps.

The next day, his first field note entry reads:

> After working in the milpa, I slept for 10 hours. I was totally exhausted, and I repeatedly dreamed of corn . . . I also remember the bees. I feel as though the perspective I had in my dream of the milpa was the perspective of a bee.

The experience of milpa farming affected the ethnographer's dreams. His experience of pain was counterbalanced by a recalcitrant desire to return to the corn of his dreamscape. An interaction with nonhumans (plants) affected his visceral responses and prompted forms of judgement that were not necessarily conscious (Coole and Frost 2010), as illustrated by the ethnographer's documentation of his own dreams. The data collector's interaction with corn initiated a process that affected his interest in, and return to, corn.

Tuning in to these experiences affected the ethnographer's diurnal rhythms. It began to make sense for him to wake up at 4:00 a.m. when the sky was black and the air was cool to walk briskly with other farmers to the milpa. Morning conversations involved farmers speaking deeply about the lunar cycle, wind patterns, cloud formations, and probabilities of rain. Walking like this during the early morning hours and filling their conversations with nonhuman topics, the tele-electronic world seemed to melt away. Some of the farmers did not have smartphones, or any phones at all.

It is common for outsiders (nonsubsistence farmers, urban Salvadorans, academics) to talk about the *machismo* (a type of performative masculinity) of Salvadoran campesinos, which often becomes conflated with the perception that campesino men (usually milpa farmers) lack formal education and good manners. While machismo is certainly present in rural El Salvador, as an analytic category it can generate shallow representations of campesinos. The trope eclipses recognition of the acute sensitivities of farmers to signals in their environments, farmers' unique perceptions of plants and their growth cycles, and the longing, dreams, and perceptions of remote sensing that farmers experience and articulate in relation to their milpas.

Mike knew about machismo, but through his interaction with plants found himself engaging in prolonged conversations with other farmers, mostly men, about the moon, plants, birds, clouds, wind, the beauty of a milpa, and their shared experience of having incessant dreams about milpas. Dreaming about corn fields is what drew the ethnographer back to corn, and dreams were a topic of conversation with milpa farmers who also dreamed about milpas. These conversations were the fodder of free associative thinking and utterances between farmers reclining in hammocks, sipping coffee, and eating at kitchen tables.

We wrote this section on field notes in the third person to clearly illustrate how field note taking, as a data collection practice, can contain data regarding more-than-human intimacies that emerge in milpa farming. Perhaps the field notes appear to be so personal that it seems like they might be more of the ethnographer's diary than a record of an external, observable "field." But the personalized field note entry emerged from the ethnographer's experience of a more-than-human assemblage, which has emergent properties that implicate human observers and observed people. After the ethnographer experienced milpa farming for several months, he worked with a broader team to survey a larger number of farmworkers in El Norteño about their experiences with more-than-human intimacies.

Questionnaires and Self-Reported Attachment, Nostalgia, and Dreaming

Below, we present findings derived from questionnaires that were administered to 128 farmworkers in El Norteño. A team of nine students from UCA El Salvador—four men and five women, most of whom were studying economics and interested in quantitative methods—assisted with administering the surveys as part of their volunteer service during their course of study at the university. The questionnaires were all administered in the Spanish language. The survey was developed after the experience of recuperative observation that was described in chapter 2. This was a grounded, ethnographically driven approach to design a questionnaire—one that might help researchers develop better numbers by exploring questions derived from ethnographic excess (Roberts 2021). Self-reported experiences with farming techniques, tools, memories of farming practice, nostalgia for seed varieties, dreams about corn and the milpa, and attachment to the harvest were some of the topics explored in the questionnaires, which would help to partially characterize the distribution of these phenomena in town. Farmers' abilities to recount their agrarian pasts and willingness to admit feeling a deep nostalgia for corn varieties from the past could lend toward the collection and analysis of data that might contain additional patterns worth considering. We would use machine learning algorithms to see what variables were most associated with "outcome" variables of interest (e.g., nostalgia for traditional corn varieties) and to reflect openly on what those quantitative findings could mean. A more technical description of the quantitative analytic methods that we used to analyze and interpret data is presented in the appendix.

To quantitatively measure self-reported intimacies with plants, farmers were asked to rate their responses to several questions using Likert scaled response sets. This means that farmers who completed the questionnaire were given a bipolar spectrum upon which they could plot a response about intimacy (e.g., 1 = I don't miss corn that was cultivated before, 2 = I miss it a little, 3 = I miss it a lot, 4 = I really miss it a lot). The point of the endeavor was not to validate the measures or place too much emphasis on differences between quantitative increments, but rather to distinguish farmers who may admit to being somewhere along a spectrum of a specific experience. For that reason, many of the quantitative representations of intimacies are presented as dichotomous (0, 1) variables. The point is not to represent nostalgia with a number, but to see how types of "admitted nostalgia" associate with other factors that we might not readily see.

Among the 128 farmworkers who were surveyed, the majority reported experiencing some type of attachment to their harvest or work, missing corn or beans that were once cultivated (but are no longer cultivated), and dreaming about corn or the milpa. All farmers (100%) reported feeling at least a little *apegado* (attached) to their harvest, and 99% felt at least a little attached to their work. The majority (84.3%) endorsed missing the corn varieties that were cultivated before but that are no longer cultivated. The majority (79.7%) also reported missing the bean varieties that were cultivated before but no longer. Most farmers (87.5%) reported dreaming about corn and 86.7% dreamed about the milpa. It is notable that strong endorsements were given for farmers always dreaming about corn or the milpa, which 42.2% and 43.8% reported, respectively (see table 3.1).

We then asked farmers to name the corn and bean varieties that they remember cultivating before but that they no longer cultivate. The varieties

TABLE 3.1 Attachment and nostalgia to subsistence farming and seed varieties, *N*=128

Self-reported characteristic	Percent	*n*
Attachment to harvest		
Feels no attachment to harvest	0.0	0
Feels little attachment to harvest	6.3	8
Feels attached to harvest	26.6	34
Feels very attached to harvest	67.2	86
Attachment to work		
Feels no attachment to work	0.8	1
Feels little attachment to work	3.1	4
Feels attached to work	27.3	35
Feels very attached to work	68.8	88
Nostalgia for corn varieties		
Cannot name any type of corn that was cultivated before but not now	5.5	7
Does not miss the corn that was cultivated before but not now	10.2	13
Misses (a little) the corn that was cultivated before but not now	27.3	35
Misses (a lot) the corn that was cultivated before but not now	27.3	35
Misses (profoundly) the corn that was cultivated before but not now	29.7	38
Nostalgia for legume varieties		
Cannot name any type of bean that was cultivated before but not now	10.2	13
Does not miss the beans that were cultivated before but not now	10.2	13
Misses (a little) the beans that were cultivated before but not now	24.2	31
Misses (a lot) the beans that were cultivated before but not now	26.6	34
Misses (profoundly) the beans that were cultivated before but not now	28.9	37
Dreams about corn		
Never dreams of corn	12.5	16
Sometimes dreams of corn	45.3	58
Always dreams of corn	42.2	54
Dreams about the milpa		
Never dreams of the milpa	13.3	17
Sometimes dreams of the milpa	43.0	55
Always dreams of the milpa	43.8	56

that farmers reported are listed in table 3.2. It is important to mention that while members of the community still cultivate many of these varieties listed, farmers may be referring to a specific subtype of a traditional variety that they no longer personally cultivate or that they may be unaware their neighbors are cultivating. Table 3.2 should be interpreted as a table of varieties associated with personal loss, not necessarily community loss. Finally, it is possible that the variety names reflect folk etymology, are misspelled, or are

TABLE 3.2 Traditional corn and seed varieties that individual farmers reported cultivating in the past but no longer cultivate

Corn	Beans	
Amarillo	Aleton	Manteca
Blanco	Arbolito	Matocho
Blanco-amarillo	Berenclengo	Mico
Capulín	Blanco	Milperos
Carjil	Castillo	Mono
Catracho (Hondureño)	Catrachino (frijol negro)	Negrito catracho
Criollo	Ceda lila	Negro/Negrito
Cuenteño	Cedon	Perendengo
Estica	Chaparrastique	Pone olla
Gigante	Chilipuca	Preseno
Indio	Cineco vaina blanca	Pupuyo
Lerdo	Colocho	San Pedrano
Liberal	Colorado	Sangre de toro
Maíz híbrido	Criollo	Sarado/Saradito
Maízon	Cuarenteño	Segoviano
Nacional	Cuarentizo	Tacetillo
Negrito/Negro	De arroz	Talete/Taletillo/Taletoyo
Obero	De ejote	Tanatillo/Taunatio vaina blanca
Raque/Reque/Roque/ Raquicito/Rocamel	De lila	Tatarata
Rosita	De seda	Tineco
Taberon/Taberito	Garbanzo	Tinto
Tulpeño	La Rienda	Tubero
Tuza morada	Liberal	Vaina blanca

intrafamilial names assigned to traditional varieties that may be duplicative. We have tried our best to re-turn and revise the lists. Regardless, we name them all here to illustrate the breadth of what was remembered and reported to data collectors.

Triads Tests

In cognitive anthropology, the triads test is an elicitation procedure that can be used to investigate local perceptions of association and difference for various items in a domain (Nazarea 1998; Nyamongo 2002; Ross, Barrientos, and Esquit-Choy 2005). In this case, local corn varieties were the domain of interest. Triads tests were conducted by randomizing corn seed varieties to farmers (e.g., maíz capulin, maíz blanco, maíz rocumel, maíz negro) on ten separate occasions per farmer. Farmers were asked to identify one variety that was unlike the other two, and then to describe why the variety was distinct. Farmers provided open-ended responses that were subsequently coded to distinguish the typology used by farmers to characterize any one variety as distinct. Here, we are not interested in the variety chosen as much as the pattern in the characterization provided by the farmer to distinguish one variety from the other two. Frequencies of distinguishing characteristics used by farmers are illustrated in table 3.3.

Gastronomic characteristics were the most frequently used to distinguish a variety of traditional corn, including references made to food that can be made with the seeds (such as tortillas and pupusas) and the relative flavor of the seed. This is notable as it reinforces a "labor of sensing that undergirds productive labor" (Kantor 2019) that occurs during milpa farming, where food preparation and vicarious intimacies shared (often with women in the home environment) affect how farmers distinguish traditional varieties. While these normative gendered representations are not deterministic or all-encompassing (rural women also farm and rural men also cook), they are nonetheless observable patterns worth mentioning as they illustrate processes of vicarious intimacy that occur between people in kitchens and during meals, which re-attune farmers' attention back to traditional cultivars conserved in-situ on milpas. This topic will be further explored in chapter 6. The abundance/growth of the cobs and seeds produced was another characteristic frequently used to distinguish a traditional corn variety. The commonality of these three characteristics underscores the subsistence orientation of the community studied, where dependence on corn harvested relates directly to local farmers' livelihoods and diets. Familiarity with the seed variety was the fourth most common characteristic, followed by morphological descriptions (including seed color and size of the cob produced by that variety).

Diagramming Activity

Diagramming activities can be used to analyze features of an item that may play major roles in peoples' daily decisions (Nazarea 1998). Participants were

TABLE 3.3 Triads test results for traditional corn seed varieties among subsistence farmworkers from Chalatenango, El Salvador, N=128

Distinguishing characteristics	Proportion of sample reporting the characteristic
Morphological	
Seed color	0.48
Seed shape	0.21
Cob color	0.16
Size of the plant	0.26
Shape of the plant	0.02
Leaf color	0.02
Size of the leaves	0.01
Texture of the cob	0.05
Size of the cob	0.41
Gastronomic	
Food that can be made with the seeds (tortillas, pupusas)	0.59
Beverages that can be made with the seeds	0.21
Texture of the seed	0.06
Flavor of the seed	0.56
Secondary effects associated with consuming the seed	0.00
Growth	
Abundance/proliferation of cobs/seeds produced	0.55
Maturation period	0.07
Abundance/proliferation of leaves	0.00
Price	0.22
Knowledge	
Familiarity with variety (well known, unknown)	0.51
Traditionality of variety (traditional, or new/not traditional)	0.07
Utility (more utilized, less utilized)	0.37
Quality	0.16
Agronomical	
Relative harvest produced	0.36
Ideal period for planting	0.00
Resistance to plagues/pests/infestations	0.09
Food for animals	0.13
Resistance to climate	0.21
Adaptation to local soil	0.04
Medicinal	
Medicinal value of husks (in food/teas)	0.00
Value of parts of the plant for food/medicine	0.10
Medicinal value of the seeds	0.04

FIGURE 3.5 A farmer uses the sickle as a straight edge to draw.

asked to separately diagram corn, beans, and squash. They were given colored pencils and multiple sheets of paper. The data collection team coded each diagram (384 diagrams total) to characterize general attributes of each drawing. Examples of diagrams are provided in figures 3.5, 3.6, and 3.7.

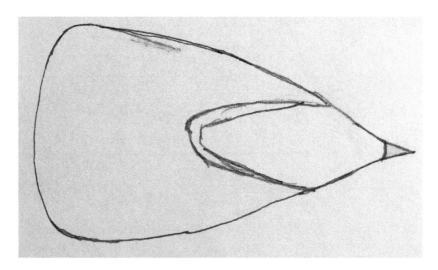

FIGURE 3.6 Corn seed drawn by farmer.

FIGURE 3.7 Ayote, or squash, drawn by farmer.

TABLE 3.4 Summaries of plant diagrams

Depicted in diagram	Corn		Beans		Squash	
	N	Percent	N	Percent	N	Percent
Seed	12	9.60	21	16.8	11	8.9
Roots present in drawing	67	65.1	42	44.2	31	48.4
Soil present in drawing	26	25.2	25	26.3	15	23.4
Multiple colors used	50	40.0	37	29.6	34	27.2

For corn diagrams, the most common type of drawing included a depiction of the plant's stalk along with a depiction of a cob covered in corn leaves ($n = 77$, 61.6%). For bean diagrams, the most common type of drawing was of a plant with a vine and a depiction of bean pods growing on the vine, but with no flowers depicted ($n = 51$, 40.8%). For squash, the most common type of plant depicted was ayote ($n = 93$, 73.8%), and the most common type of drawing included a depiction of the fruit ($n = 48$, 38.7%). For each type of plant drawn, whether the participant drew the seed, whether roots were present in the drawing, whether the soil was demarcated, and whether multiple colors were used for a particular plant were coded. Results for these diagram attributes are shown in table 3.4. Taken together, corn was the plant where diagrams most frequently included the roots and use of multiple colors to depict the plant.

Quantitative Analyses

We used random forest algorithms (a machine learning technique) to understand what variables were closely aligned with intimacy variables in the farmer questionnaires. Variables that tended to show the greatest levels of association with the intimacies examined were the number of subsistence farmers in a farmer's network, the farmer's time spent living in the area where the survey was conducted, and the age and education level of the farmer. When it came to nostalgia and dreaming about corn, self-reported attachments to the harvest and the work of subsistence farming were particularly important.

Each of the intimacy variables examined has complex, intersecting, quantitative interactions with the variables we describe above, and for sake of brevity we will not review each. We will instead focus on examples that illustrate concepts discussed in the vignette about Gerardo. Here, we focus on in-situ cultivation of a traditional seed variety and dreaming about the milpa.

For in-situ conservation of a traditional corn variety, 55.5% of farmers reported cultivating a traditional variety of corn. We think about Gerardo and the multiple traditional seed cultivars (varieties produced by selective breeding) of corn that he gifted to people in the community and research-ers alike—varieties that did not have alphanumeric names but names like maíz criollo amarillo. Random forest algorithms helped us identify that the following variables were deemed to be closely related to the practice of in-situ corn conservation among farmers who completed the questionnaire in El Norteño: age of the farmworker, education level, time lived in the town, nostalgia for corn varieties, and the number of farmers in the individual's network. Of all the nonlinear effects we subsequently examined, the inter-action between nostalgia for corn varieties of the past and the age of the farmworker were the most related. Upon further examination, farmers who reported the greatest/most profound levels of nostalgia for corn varieties of the past were most likely to be cultivating a traditional variety in-situ. Farm-ers under the age of forty who also reported intense nostalgia were the most likely to be cultivating an in-situ variety. These machine learning findings reflect back to the research team the inherent biases of the ethnographer studying intimacy, who was under forty at the time of data collection, who assembled with other farmworkers (around his age), and who was theoret-ically sampling on nostalgia. This final point brings us back to recuperative observation and the key informant farmers who taught the researcher what they knew about the milpa. The algorithm reflected a preexisting bias that nonetheless drove the ethnographic research forward. Within the sample, younger farmers (<forty years of age) with intense nostalgia for seed va-rieties of the past were the most likely to be conserving traditional corn varieties in-situ. They were also the farmers who taught the ethnographer to farm traditional corn, who gave him the ideas for the survey that was con-structed, and who shared their traditional corn seeds. The algorithms reflect characteristics of the participant observer at the time data were collected, revealing something more about the method, perhaps, than they do about more-than-human intimacies. Algorithmic bias entails systematic deviation from a standard, and in this case the algorithms inherited bias from data the algorithms were trained on without influence from the programmer/

ethnographer who ran the algorithms, but rather the theoretical sampling and first-hand experience he built the questionnaire upon (Castro, O'Brien, and Schwan 2023; Castro 2022). By re-turning data derived from questionnaires, we return to and re-turn the conditions that produced recuperative observation to understand the results.

Corn farming drew the ethnographer in through the dreams that he had immediately following his time in the field. For a participant observer, this can be a personally important experience as well as an experience that helps in sharing a common and intimate grounding for conversations with other farmers. Farmers who felt very attached to their harvest were more likely to dream about their milpa. This relationship between harvest attachment and dreaming was particularly strong for older farmers (greater than seventy years of age) and younger farmers (less than forty years of age). Less formal education was associated with more dreaming about the milpa. This relationship was most distinct among those who felt most attached to their milpa. Generally, farmers who claimed to have a larger network of subsistence farmers tended to dream more frequently about the milpa. If we think about Gerardo who dreamed about his milpa, almost seeing what would happen to the plants before it did, he had very little formal education but incredible attachment to his milpa. Gerardo was generous and openly shared seeds with new acquaintances and outsiders, easily forming bonds and expanding the size of his network of farmers predicated upon his enthusiasm for farming that he shared with other farmers in processes of vicarious intimacy. This is one of the spaces in which more-than-human intimacies could be re-turned through code. Findings also illustrate some pathways through which vicarious intimacies travel away from the milpa and through people who return to and re-turn the milpa during rainy seasons in the rural north.

The quantitative data above illustrate some crude ways of measuring and reporting more-than-human intimacies and help us understand some of the "variables" that are associated with self-reported intimacies as measured through questionnaires. Structured questionnaires can be useful, but they are also highly restrictive and place strict limits on the participant's voice. The descriptive data produced by ethnography informed the development of the questionnaire, and ethnographic data aid us in interpreting the quantitative results. The mixed methods approach was not intended to "triangulate" a concept, but rather to further explore findings derived from recuperative observation. In considering multiple methods, we also recognize "the tainted nature of all method" (Bubandt, Andersen, and Cypher 2022, 10) and the human biases they have a tendency of reflecting in the study of emergent properties of more-than-human assemblages. The jump from qualitative methods (participant observation / recuperative observation) to quantitative methods (questionnaires analyzed with statistical methods) partially characterized the distribution of these phenomena in El Norteño. The findings can help us understand the concept of more-than-human intimacies that arise between farmers and milpas in Chalatenango, as well as strengths and limitations of methodologies used to understand more-than-human intimacies.

Conclusion

In this chapter on more-than-human intimacies, we heard a brief and focused story of Gerardo, who practices in-situ conservation of traditional seed varieties, and whose poetic description of his relationship with his milpa invites us deeper into his experience of conserving chilipuca beans and traditional corn varieties. Then, we illustrated an embodied example derived from the ethnographer's field notes. Finally, we analyzed some quantitative data derived from questionnaires, triads tests, and diagrams that show how intimacies of interest may be distributed in a corn farming community. The numbers are meant to help us think about patterns associated with the phenomenon of interest, as well as patterns that reflect methodological biases. Both should be taken into account to understand more-than-human intimacies, which affect farmers. More-than-human intimacies can also affect those who research these intimacies, directly and/or through processes of vicarious intimacy with other milpa farmers.

We characterize more-than-human intimacies as emergent properties of more-than-human assemblages (DeLanda 2006; Bennett 2010, 24). The intimacies are something felt, detected, and reported by farmers in relation to something that is not human. More-than-human intimacies emerge from human experiences with plants and re-attune people back to milpas and the plants within them that are the objects of human longing and dreaming. More-than-human intimacies are characterized by everyday attunements to, sensitivities regarding, and affectively charged experiences of nonhumans in more-than-human assemblages (Anastario et al. 2021a). The figure of enchantment is bidirectional, pointing toward the humans who feel enchantment and the nonhumans that produce effects in human and other bodies (Bennett 2010, xii). Corn, bean, and squash plants assemble with milpa farmers who cultivate them, eat them, save their seeds, and transmit those seeds between humans over multiple rainy seasons. Theoretically, the more-than-human intimacies that farmers experience implicate both material (capacities for emoting and perceiving) and expressive (linguistic) components of assemblages. The intimacies are more-than-human because they involve a sense of human intimacy that is conjugated with plants and that does something; it produces agency implicated in the regeneration of the milpa each year. Our findings bear some similarity with those described by Sophie Chao in her research on the multispecies entanglements of oil palm plantations in West Papua, where Chao describes affectively and morally charged labors of care surrounding sago palm. Chao (2022, 119–20) describes "being in the grove" as involving a range of affective and embodied interactions between sago, humans, and other collaborators. The multispecies encounter produces attunements across species lines (Chao 2022, 120). In our research, seed varieties were longed for, corn fields were dreamed about, and longing and dreaming were entwined with the in-situ conservation of traditional cultivars.

While there is a great deal of quantitative data presented in this chapter, it is important to emphasize that more-than-human intimacies emerged as a topic of interest by the ethnographer first directly experiencing the intimacies and reflecting upon them. This became apparent through the collection of field notes, which informed the development of a questionnaire, a triads test, and a diagramming activity that would be administered to farmers at a later point in time. Recuperative observation both preceded the quantitative method and aided in the interpretation of the quantitative results. Human bias is infused in the research methods presented. Much like farmers who spend long periods of time observing and interacting with plants, reflecting upon their growth, dreaming about them, and talking to them, the experience of participant observation with corn farmers gave rise to ethnographic experiences with these intimacies through the practice of farming. Recognizing and harnessing ethnographic data led to a certain type of quantitative approach that could be refined to explore and understand patterns in something that might feel obvious to the ethnographer but, simultaneously, feel ineffable and difficult to grasp. Mixing methods, in this context, helped us to name something that can be revisited and returned in future studies of more-than-human assemblages, acknowledging and working with (as opposed to escaping) the human biases that haunt our ways of knowing.

FOUR

Agrichemicals in an Agrarian Assemblage

Methodologies for Documenting Memories of Nonhumans

Synopsis

This chapter focuses on methods for eliciting information about nonhumans in the life histories of farmers. It illustrates how ethnographic insights can drive methodological advances concerning personal histories of aggregate and cumulative exposures. It focuses on a single class of nonhuman actants—in this case, agrichemicals. It draws from and builds upon methods for eliciting agrarian life and community histories (Nazarea, 1998, 2005) and Elizabeth Roberts' (2021) development of bioethnography. The methodological development described here reflects a process that began with participant observation and ended with life history calendars quantitatively encoding memories of milpa farmers' interactions with agrichemicals across the lifespan.

Narrating the Exposome

Alejandro, a young Salvadoran farmer with kidney problems, was sweating under the brutal midday sun. He asked the ethnographer a haunting question:

"¿Los químicos están matando a la gente . . . vea?"

"The chemicals are killing people . . . right?"

The conversation had originally been focused on Alejandro's cultivation of traditional seed varieties, but this morbid detour was one that began repeating itself as the ethnographer became more attuned to the everyday concerns of Salvadoran milpa farmers.

The question about whether the agrichemicals were killing farmers was a signal that there was much more than botanical actants that weighed on farmers' minds in the more-than-human assemblage of milpa farming. The question about everyday chemicals killing people, something that the ethnographer was not originally focused on as part of this work, began to haunt him. Avery Gordon (2008) describes a haunting as "when what's been in your blind spot comes into view." In this case, the ample off-label use of agrichemicals, memories about them, and their perceived toxicity was coming into the ethnographer's view as he had been myopically focused on intimacies associated with the in-situ conservation of traditional cultivars, almost to a fault. The farmer was not necessarily referencing a single exposure to a single chemical, but the aggregate, cumulative, and temporal increase in the use of multiple agrichemicals that he, and many others, had observed over the course of recent history.

We take farmers' observations of their everyday exposures seriously and think about ways to harness what is learned through repeated observations of peoples' everyday intimacies and activities to inform quantitative measurement of cumulative agrichemical exposures across the lifespan. Milpa farmers use and often rely on sharp observations over time and rainy seasons to inform their own decision-making about what actions to take on a milpa during the current iteration of the rainy season. Milpa farmers' observations of agrichemicals were pointed and troubling. Farmers' observations provoked a slow and nonlinear line of methodological development, described in this chapter, inspired by their attention to technological developments and emergent health issues in their everyday lives. Grounded in ethnography, the process by which the methods and data collection instruments were developed are closely aligned with and informed by Elizabeth Roberts' bioethnographic approach, which explores the articulation of ethnographic and biostatistical data in symmetrical analyses to understand the relational and contingent phenomena of environment-body interactions (Roberts and Sanz 2018; Roberts 2019). Roberts describes how bioethnography "harnesses ethnographic excess to make better numbers, numbers better situated within the reality they purport to represent" (Roberts 2021). In our case, the sequential development and evaluation of methods aimed at measuring human-chemical interactions narrated by farmworkers stemmed directly from qualitative data, where agrichemicals appeared and reappeared in field notes, transcripts, and the dozens of unrecorded conversations about what might be causing excess disease burdens for farmers. It is an endeavor that is informed by an "epistemic demeanor of participants as knowers" (Verran 2018, 127), where ethnographic data eventually inform the development of instruments that are notorious for producing "thin description" through numbers (Jackson 2013, 13). This chapter illustrates the ways in which a grounded imperative to understand farmers' stories about agrichemicals of the past and present can drive the design and use of methods that articulate what was learned through qualitative findings with quantitative approaches to retrospective exposure assessment in an attempt to "make better numbers" (Roberts 2021). Since this chapter is focused on methods that are used to understand human-chemical interactions that occur, that are remembered, and that are retold across the human lifespan, the remainder of this introduction will briefly provide the reader with some additional context to understand the urgency with which these stories are being told by Salvadoran farmers who cultivate milpas.

In El Salvador, the emergence of chronic kidney disease of unknown origin (CKDu, also referred to as Mesoamerican nephropathy) coincided with the maturation of the Green Revolution that was described in chapter 1. The deployment of chemically intensive modern agricultural technologies to low-income countries that occurred during this period was like a type of "biopiracy," where the influx of agrichemicals generated improvements for many while simultaneously intensifying patterns of traditional discrimination and exploitation (Braidotti 2010), in this case among Salvadoran farmers. The cultural shifts away from fire and fallow farming methods and increasing imports of pesticides correlated with increased deaths due to pesticide poisoning in the Central American region, with some of the highest per capita rates observed in El Salvador in the late twentieth century (PAHO 2002; MSPAS 1999, 2000a, 2000b; Alfaro de Hidalgo 2014). This is one of the ways in which agriculture implicates intimate relationships, particularly concerning the death of various organisms that are targeted or not targeted by the chemicals (Hetherington 2020, 188). Since the 1990s, there has been an increase in CKDu, which is kidney disease not associated with known risk factors (hypertension, diabetes, heart disease, obesity), and which disproportionately affects younger men who work in agriculture (Orantes Navarro et al. 2014; Orantes Navarro et al. 2015; Herrera-Valdés et al. 2014; Laws et al. 2015; Brooks, Ramirez-Rubio, Amador 2012). CKDu is suspected to arise from a multifactorial interplay of lifestyle, environmental and occupational exposures, genetic variation, and infections (Mendley et al. 2019; Martín-Cleary and Ortiz 2014; Johnson, Wesseling, and Newman 2019). While evidence is accumulating that heat stress plays a role in renal function decline (Roncal-Jimenez et al. 2015; Gallo-Ruiz et al. 2019; Peraza et al. 2012; Athuraliya et al. 2011), the role of agrichemical exposures (alone, or in combination with other factors such as heat) is poorly understood. Whether agrichemicals play a role in this particular disease is not what motivates this chapter; the fact that milpa farmers suspect that agrichemicals play a role in their health outcomes (like CKDu and death) is why we re-turn methodological attention on the agrichemicals imbricated in milpa farmers' rural lifeways.

Pesticides commonly used by Salvadoran subsistence farmers today, including the herbicides glyphosate and paraquat and the insecticide parathion (Anastario et al. 2021b; Todd 2021a, 184), are known to cause kidney injury and damage. In a case-control study of paddy farmers in the dry zone of Sri Lanka, the highest risk of CKDu was observed among participants who drank abandoned well water containing high glyphosate levels and among participants who sprayed glyphosate (Jayasumana et al. 2015). Glyphosate, originally patented for its feature of being a strong chelator of heavy metals (Mesnage et al. 2015), may transport metals to the kidney (Gunatilake, Seneff, and Orlando 2019; Babich et al. 2020). Glyphosate and its formulations can also cause oxidative stress, leading to organ damage (Mesnage et al. 2015). Case studies of glyphosate poisoning have found unspecified renal failure and acute kidney injury in patients (Scammell et al. 2019).

Paraquat is an herbicide that milpa farmers often use to clear the field of weeds before planting corn. Paraquat was examined among pesticide applicators in the Agricultural Health Study, where significant positive associations were detected between end-stage renal disease and intensity-weighted cumulative use of several herbicides including paraquat, compared to no use (Lebov et al. 2016). Among Agricultural Health Study participants' wives who never applied pesticides, the risk of end-stage renal disease was associated with their husbands having ever used paraquat (Lebov et al. 2015). In patients with paraquat poisoning, acute kidney injury is common (McClean et al. 2010; Kim et al. 2009), and fatal poisoning has been shown to cause tubular degeneration in the kidneys and necrosis of the proximal tubules (Scammell et al. 2019).

Parathion is an insecticide that subsistence farmers sprinkle directly onto corn seeds stored between rainy seasons, and/or may be placed inside of perforated tin cans used in home grain silos, presenting the possibility of accidental inhalation and ingestion. In a cross-sectional epidemiological study conducted in El Salvador among 2,388 persons living in agricultural communities, CKD was associated with methyl parathion contact (Orantes Navarro et al. 2014). In a case study of parathion intoxication, patient symptoms were suggestive of hepatitis along with acute kidney injury (Vikrant 2015).

While glyphosate, paraquat, and parathion are pesticides of interest in the study of CKDu, research is inconclusive as to whether prolonged and repeated exposure to these agrichemicals is associated with renal function decline. Mixed results from short-term and cross-sectional studies suggest that research on cumulative lifetime exposures is necessary to better understand the role of chronic exposures on a chronic disease, specifically CKDu risk (Scammell et al. 2019; Valcke et al. 2017). This is not to say that agrichemicals are directly causing CKDu, but the temporal co-occurrence of pesticide poisonings, studies documenting their nephrotoxic effects, and farmers witnessing the effects of pesticides have deeply affected farmers who wonder, often, about what all the agrichemicals in their lifeways are doing to the soil, seeds, bodies, and local environment. When milpa farmers wonder aloud if their everyday chemical use is what is killing people, we believe it is worth dedicating methodological attention to this everyday hypothesis.

Regardless of the etiological role that agrichemicals may play in CKDu, the everyday hypothesis that agrichemicals are killing farmers is often predicated on the observation that farmers have interacted with these chemicals in ways that evade how people who do not work in agriculture, such as doctors (and by extension, epidemiologists and health researchers), ask questions about them. This is one way in which milpa farmers have experienced the slow violence associated with the increasing ubiquity of agrichemicals in their lifeways, undergoing sporadic science about their routines and, in most cases, no science at all (Hetherington 2020, 168; Tousignant 2018, 9; Nixon 2011, 2). Sleeping next to agrichemicals during the entire span of one's childhood, or accidentally and repeatedly ingesting agrichemicals while eating breakfast on the milpa, are not typical exposures that are measured (or even considered) when scientists attempt to reconstruct an exposure history. But when farmers tell stories about these everyday exposures, they are narrating components of their "exposome," which in the environmental health sciences is referred to as "the cumulative measure of environmental influences and associated biological responses throughout the lifespan including exposures from the environment, diet, behavior, and endogenous processes" (Miller and Jones 2014; Wild 2005; Miller 2020, 3). One of the critical aspects of this definition of the exposome is its focus on the "cumulative measure," suggesting that "if there is no current (or in development) means of measuring the component, then it cannot be part of the entity" (Miller 2020, 3). Self-report or direct observation by an ethnographer may be noisy and troublesome measures when compared with those typically used by environmental health scientists, but these measures can simultaneously expand an understanding of how, where, and why environmental influences occur. Another critical aspect of the exposome definition is its focus on human behaviors. Ethnographers conducting studies in agrarian lifeways can contribute ample data that inform the measurement of everyday behaviors and perceived toxicities of chemical components on the human body, providing culturally informative data regarding exposomes in populations, subpopulations, and communities. While these qualitative insights may not readily translate to quantitative metrics considered reliable, valid, or generalizable for scientists who study the exposome, the observations are nonetheless troublesome and carry the potential to reshape how the exposome of a group of people suffering excess disease burdens is conceptualized and measured in relation to social and cultural processes.

This chapter draws upon methods of life history elicitation to argue for articulative, cross-disciplinary, slow-moving methodological advances grounded in and driven by farmers' insights into their relationships with agrichemicals across the lifespan. It draws directly from participant observation, in-depth interviews, life history matrices used in reconstructive memory banking procedures in cultural anthropology (Nazarea 1998, 27–28), and life history calendars (Freedman et al. 1988; Glasner and van der Vaart 2009) to imperfectly develop methodologies that advance lines of inquiry grounded in farmers' observations and everyday health concerns. It narrates a methodological development driven by an ethical imperative to respond, even if in an imperfect way, to farmers like Alejandro when they ask the outsider gringo academic researcher the haunting question of whether the chemicals are killing people. As an outsider researcher with access to the internet and science, shouldn't he know? The farmers' stories are worth taking seriously, and there is more than one method of recognizing patterns in these stories. This chapter describes and illustrates those methods that hold promise for expanding and informing an understanding of the context in which environmental influences occur for milpa farmers.

Field Notes

As a method, participant observation offers a unique way of documenting everyday life that is unlike other methods available to scientists across numerous other disciplines. Virginia Nazarea reminds anthropologists that "beyond mediating or brokering, anthropologists can try to penetrate and articulate the sand in, as well as the rubber on, other people's shoes—or non-shoes—because we are presented with multiple opportunities for getting as close as possible to walking in them" (2014).

As a participant observer who was trying to focus on more-than-human intimacies between plants and people, the ethnographer's field notes were full of instances where brief mention was given to a discarded herbicide label he found while working in a cornfield, insecticides stored in sleeping quarters, and nitrogen/phosphorous/potassium fertilizer mixtures that stained the palms of his hands neon pink, causing them to swell to the point that it was difficult to write field notes. Those field notes also document troubling stories about kids who became "drunk" on cypermethrin while helping their families plant sorghum, and conversations about grandparents who quickly died after adopting the use of backpack pumps to spray paraquat to clear the weeds on their milpas. A farmer who endearingly called the ethnographer *chele* (whitey) committed suicide by swallowing an aluminum phosphide tablet used as rodenticide for corn grain stores. Agrichemicals were ubiquitous in the space of more-than-human intimacies, and they did drastic, sometimes lethal things to the people and plants that were entangled with them. Below are some examples of how field notes and in-depth interviews used in the context of participant observation elucidated these everyday exposures that occurred for farmers over time.

Agrichemicals appeared in the ethnographer's field notes before he had any interest in agrichemicals. One day before planting corn with a farmer, the ethnographer wrote the following into his fieldnotes:

We will clean . . . with a cuma ("sickle"), and then put down paraquat, which has a label that says it contains 1,1'—dimethyl-4, 4'-bipryidinium 20%. It is an herbicide. [The farmer] put it into a 4-gallon bomba ("pump") (4 lid servings in 4 gallons of water) and afterward fumigated the terrain . . . says it takes about 2–3 days to kill the weeds . . . I talk with [the farmer] about taking pictures, and he wants to make sure that his face never appears in any picture of anything related to growing corn.

September 19, 2017

It stopped raining and [the farmer] told me he was going to fumigate. I was standing back from the second plot and the stench of the fumigation was overwhelming . . . the smell of the chemical was overwhelming.

September 24, 2017

In the field notes above, the ethnographer had little understanding of what paraquat was before he used it, but he wrote it down in his field notes as he encountered it in its everyday use, including the waste that he found in and around milpas (see figure 4.1). The ethnographer also documented how paraquat was applied by milpa farmers, with limited attention to the direction of the wind or the use of personal protective equipment. Exposure

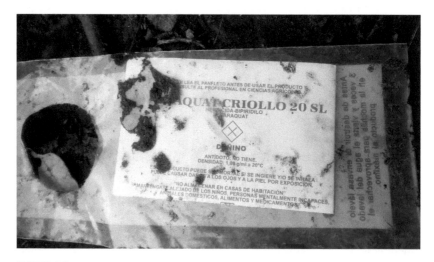

FIGURE 4.1 Discarded paraquat label found on the soil of a milpa.

to pesticide drift happens regularly among farmers who are not pesticide applicators or mixers, but it is an underdocumented and understudied phenomenon (Guthman 2019, 148; Anastario et al. 2022a). The ethnographer never encountered milpa farmers using personal protective equipment when applying agrichemicals, but sometimes found that they washed their hands in rivers before eating breakfast on the milpa or tied bandanas or T-shirts around their faces to act as makeshift respirators when experiencing pesticide drift (this does not adequately protect farmers from inhaling toxic insecticides and herbicides nor does it protect from dermal absorption).

What is important to understand from the field notes above is that the farmer and the ethnographer were not using paraquat according to the label's instructions. In rural El Salvador, this was everyday milpa farming practice. The chemical might be strong, but it was being used to do something else (kill weeds) with little attention given to how it might be affecting those farming the milpa at the time of its application. Tolerating the effect of the agrichemical exposure was sometimes conflated with masculinity and/or Indigeneity (note, this was not always the case, and many farmers explicitly expressed concern surrounding their use). Mike was often told to stay away from paraquat mist because he lacked *Indio* (Indian) blood, suggesting that his lack of Indigenous ancestry made him less capable of tolerating pesticide exposures. Becoming drenched in paraquat, becoming dizzy from inhaling it, and becoming sick after a day applying it were everyday discomforts associated with modern milpa farming. But of all the things that farmers are exposed to (high temperatures, snakes, wasps, infectious disease, contaminated water), many wondered what these chemicals were doing to them in the long run.

What is also telling about the field notes is how the farmer did not want his picture taken because he was ashamed of being represented as a corn farmer. Publicly, the farmer maintained an identity as a construction worker, and he felt a sense of stigma about being identified as a corn farmer. Construction workers are typically treated as an occupational class that is distinct from farm workers in epidemiological studies of CKDu, and it is possible that quantitative models that categorize individuals as construction workers may overlook milpa farming practices among construction workers. While the interaction offers an important lesson about photos and representation, it also underscores the marginalization and ongoingness of the milpa in Salvadoran society. As discussed in chapter 1, milpa farming has always been at the margins of the history of Salvadoran agriculture, despite being one of the longest-standing agricultural practices that we know of in the space of El Salvador. Milpa farming can also be invisible to scientists responsible for measuring exposure to agrichemicals among occupational classes where participants do not identify as farmers. Participant observation can be useful in identifying "who" is exposed to "what," "when," and "how" as milpa farmers engage in other occupations and migrate to the United States. Participant observation offers insights into these everyday practices that may evade self-reported information regarding occupation on questionnaires used by scientists who are concerned with environmental exposures. They can capture fragments of data that count "edges of exposure," where chemicals with known toxicity circulate but which evade epidemiological surveys and monitoring routines (Tousignant 2018, 5). Everyday exposures are accessible to participant observers who document these occurrences in agrarian lifeways.

Narratives of Everyday Exposures and In-depth Interviews

In everyday conversations, milpa farmers narrated community and personal histories of agrichemical use. The types of chemicals used, the patterns of their use, and the effects they had on soils and bodies change rapidly in these stories because so many living farmers were children during the implementation of the Green Revolution and its wake. In-depth, open-ended interviews allow farmers to narrate stories about their observations and use of agrichemicals over the life course in nonlinear ways. Farmers who articulated their more-than-human intimacies with the Salvadoran milpa often told stories, remembered, and theorized about the constellation of agrichemicals that have flowed through their lifeways since the 1950s (which reflects the earliest memories among the farmers interviewed for this project). While the Chalateco farmers we interviewed did not claim Indigenous identity (but often claimed having Indigenous blood or being *Indio*), the ways in which farmers told stories bore semblance to Indigenous methodologies such as storytelling and remembering that are both method and meaning (Smith 2012). Stories generate knowledge about places and time frames that get transmitted orally. Sometimes these stories contain information about agrichemicals that come and go from lifeways, but that people remember for certain reasons.

For example, Alejandro wondered about specific stints he had with specific agrichemicals during various windows of his lifespan. Here, he recounts a brief encounter with the insecticide Karate:

Pues a mí me dice que todo eso pueda ser que esté afectando dicen, si me dicen algunos "pueden ser que los venenos sean los que te afecten" sí, porque yo utilice Karate una vez porque compro los, los litros, los compro y los dejo al próximo año y cuando lo andaba regando con la bomba el frijol sentía que me venía el aire encima de mí y todo esto me picaba sí, y el cuerpo todo me picaba, dejé de tirar eso mejor. ¡N,hombre! le dije yo a la persona "ese volado pica" mejor lo deje, lo boté, sí porque vi que mucho picaba, sí porque es bueno esa, ese veneno es bueno pero mucho picaba, lo dejé, mejor de tirarlo.

Well, it shows me that all of this may be having some type of effect. Yes, some say to me that "it may be that the poisons are what are affecting you" yeah, because I used Karate once. I bought a few liters of it, and the next year when I was applying it to the beans with the pump I felt it mist me and it caused me to itch, my whole body itched, I figured better to get rid of it, no man, I told the person I was working with "that thing makes me itch," I told him it's better to get rid of it. I threw it away, because I saw how it stung a lot, because yes it's good, that poison is good but it stings a lot and it's just better to throw it away.

Alejandro is recalling event-specific knowledge about a general event (Karate exposure) during a life period in his autobiographical memory (Conway and Pleydell-Pierce 2000). Finding and developing contextual anchors that help to elicit that recalled experience of a specific agrichemical exposure, however, is a methodological process that can be informed by both participant observation and in-depth interviews practiced in the context of ethnographic research. During the rainy season, fertilizer is distributed by municipal offices, and farmers budget for and immediately secure fertilizers before sowing seeds. Even if there is no money for more expensive herbicides, fertilizers play a central role in growing corn on soil that has been reused for more than two years. Fertilizers are a type of "chemical rent" (Münster 2022, 137) that must be accounted for to grow the milpa in most contemporary milpa farming practice. While epidemiologists and toxicologists may pay little attention to fertilizers because they are not presumed to be nearly as toxic as herbicides or insecticides, farmers pay a great deal of attention to fertilizers that drive the corn growth cycle. For example, using nitrogen/phosphorous/potassium at planting, ammonium sulphate at four weeks, and urea at seven weeks of the corn growth cycle may be a gold standard that farmers delineate and budget for before factoring in herbicides such as paraquat, glyphosate, or atrazine. Farmers can distinguish the fertilizers that they have used over time and have unique ways of referencing fertilizer application. Below, another farmer, Fernando, talks about the way he balances his preferred fertilization sequence using N/P/K ("triple 15") and ammonium sulphate given what he can afford.

> En los terrenos triple quince o formula o sulfato ahí funcionan igual porque yo a la primera le pongo unos granitos de formula o sea triple quince funciona igual . . . después de la segunda lo puede usar otra vez, pero ya va mezclado con el sulfato mitad y mitad . . . le echo una cucharada de uno y otra cucharada del otro, pero yo lo mezclo todo en el saco así. Y la tercera si uso sulfato. Para el producto dice solo sulfato, solo sulfato, pero en el terreno donde yo trabajo, aunque sea dos abonadas sale el maíz, pero yo le doy tres de preferencia si puedo.

> On the land, triple fifteen, or formula, or sulphate work the same. The first thing I do is I put some granules of formula or triple fifteen, which work the same . . . after the second [fertilization] you can use it again, but you have to mix it with the sulphate, half and half . . . I put one spoonful of one, and one spoonful of the other, but I mix everything in the sack. And for the third [fertilization] I use sulphate. The product says only sulphate, only sulphate, but on the land where I work, although two fertilizations will make the corn grow, I prefer to give it three if I can.

Fernando went on to explain how his uncles only used to use ammonium sulphate, back before the other fertilizers became widely available in town. Fernando's uncles taught him to mix ash into synthetic fertilizer to treat the corn for stripes that appeared on the leaves due to nutrient deficiency. This practice is also observed contemporaneously by older farmers who mix ash with ammonium sulphate during the second fertilization of their milpitas that are kept in the same space as home gardens, much like Chepe whose story was told in the opening vignette of the Introduction of this book.

In the following interview excerpt, Gerardo described his use of the herbicides paraquat, hedonal, and gesaprim (atrazine), anchoring all of them to sequences of fertilization driving the corn growth cycle.

Mire yo uso paraquat, uso lo que es lo que preparo en la tierra, uso paraquat queda la tierra limpia así y siembro maíz sea capulín, o sea taberon, o sea H5, o maíz amarillo porque me gusta tener esa variedad por comer y la otra parte de producción porque yo el maíz amarrillo lo tengo para comer verde, en elote y entonces después de eso cuando la milpita está así, va 12 días de nacida cuando de 12 días que sembré está nacido le meto hedonal y gesaprim. . . . yo solo desde que empecé a trabajar, yo solo lo usaba pero en ocasiones porque de 3 años, de 5 años para acá he usado el gesaprim antes no lo usaba solo usaba el gramoxone pero cuando la milpa vi que se me llenaba de monte así, entonces me dijeron usa gesaprim, yo compre gesaprim le eché junto con el herbicida que es un hedonal entonces le revuelvo allí y voy despacio encima del maíz porque esa no le hace nada al maíz . . . con el hedonal agarra . . . como en una energía entonces después va el abono un poquito de químico que se le pondrá una poco entonces se va creciendo como a la primera, después la segunda como le eché gesaprim está limpia no ha nacido semilla de maleza aun el zacate sí pero la maleza no.

Look, I use paraquat, I use it to prepare the soil, I use paraquat to clean the soil and then I plant corn, it could be capulin, taberon, H5, or yellow corn because I like to have that variety to eat, and the other part is for production. I eat yellow corn when it's green, on the cob, and so after the milpa is clean, 12 days after the corn sprouts, 12 days later I put down hedonal and gesaprim. . . . Ever since I've begun to work, I only used it on occasion because for the last 3 years, I mean 5 years ago I have used gesaprim but before that I only used gramoxone. But when I saw the milpa filling up with weeds, they told me to use gesaprim, so I bought gesaprim and I put it down along with the herbicide hedonal. So, I mix it and I go putting slowly on top of the corn. It doesn't do anything to the corn. . . . With the hedonal it gets a type of energy and

so after fertilizing with a little bit of chemicals it starts to grow, after
the second [fertilization] I put gesaprim and it's clean and none of the
seeds of the weed grow. Sometimes grass grows but not other weeds.

These interview excerpts are brief glimpses of the everyday, logical ways in
which milpa farmers talk about, articulate, narrate, and recall several of the
major agrichemicals they have come into contact with over their lifespans,
and how they factor into everyday decisions about using agrichemicals on
milpas. Fertilizers have changed with time, and fertilizers drive the corn
growth cycle. Fertilizers serve as an anchor for remembering the sequence of
agrichemical use in a given rainy season. This is important to highlight given
that questionnaires that are designed to ask farmers about their exposure
to particularly toxic herbicides or insecticides may benefit from anchoring
recall of a specific chemical to the primary role that fertilizers play in con-
temporaneous cultivation practices among milpa farmers.

Life History Matrices and Questionnaires

Eliciting life histories regarding human-chemical interactions can be an engaging, cathartic, and generative task for both the interviewee and interviewer. While the collection of life history data can be largely exploratory,
it is helpful to think through how life history data will be analyzed by the
person making the effort to collect data. Adding more structure to the elic-
itation/data recording process can sometimes feel too rigid, but an instrument that permits the elicitation of unstructured accounts, coupled with
some of the structure of instruments that quantify farmers' responses, can
be used to identify patterns that may be difficult to see with an otherwise
purely inductive data collection and analysis strategy.

The point of quantifying self-reported agrichemical exposures, in this
context, is to assist researchers with the recognition of patterns that may
occur in more-than-human assemblages and in milpa farmers' exposomes.
The gradient of unstructured-to-structured methods that will be briefly reviewed here include life history matrices (qualitatively analyzed), questionnaires (analyzed with multivariable models), and life history calendars. As
we increasingly move into more structured gradients of interview procedures, we remember that structure is historically associated with relations
of epistemic power that have disproportionately valued notions of validity

built on assumptions of universality (Grosfoguel 2013). We acknowledge that more structure implies more influence of the researcher on defining the parameters of what information is captured from a willing teller of a life story, but we also acknowledge that more structure assists with the quantitative articulation of experiences among people experiencing hazards in their environments that are the objects of study. Quantitative articulation may be informative to the environmental health sciences, where chemical mixtures and lagged mixture effects are modeled to understand how environments influence human disease outcomes. The idea is not to generalize or validate, but to think about different ways for identifying patterns evident in ethnographic data that can be recalled in not only collective memory but autobiographical memory of lifetime periods and events, and then effectively communicating these findings to scientists across disciplines.

Life History Matrices

Life history matrices are tables that collect information about different domains over the passage of the individual's lifespan. They allow for a re-construction of "history from below" (Nazarea 1998, 27–28). They offer an inherently interactive method and depend largely on the style of the interviewer. In using life history matrices to structure an interview, Virginia Nazarea describes a need to first outline desired information, choose key informants, and create an interview dynamic that allows for an interplay between free narration and redirecting the participant back to the information that one is seeking. Nazarea (1998, 28) provides a suggested use of a matrix for life history elicitation that involves placing temporal frames (childhood, youth, maturity, old age) as the rows in a matrix, and domains (land preparation, source of planting materials, cultural management, pest control, and post-harvest practices) as the columns. Nazarea (1998, 28) illustrated how these matrices elicited information regarding sweet potato cultivation relative to the lunar cycle, location of the crop, ethnomedicine, and disappearance of traditional cultivars.

Conducting life history matrix activities with participants aided the ethnographer's understanding of the narratives of how lifeways had dramatically shifted over time and helped him identify when specific agrichemicals appeared in the community. For example, using life history matrices with a few older respondents who had locally farmed the land illustrated how ammonium sulphate was one of the first fertilizers to begin flowing into El Norteño in the 1950s and 1960s as outside "brigades," including foreigners, taught young children how to fertilize corn varieties with alphanumeric names. It also helped illustrate that the herbicide paraquat was introduced prior to glyphosate, which became available and accessible in the local market in 2008. Life history matrices helped to elucidate themes and dates concerning agricultural practices and technologies in the area being studied. One challenge of the life history matrices involved participants with varying definitions of lifetime periods and the events occurring within those periods. For example, older participants who only attended primary school might have considered adulthood arriving at an earlier chronological age than younger participants (at the time of interview) who had completed secondary school. Older milpa farmers also tended to believe that their lifespans would be shorter, whereas younger milpa farmers expected to live longer lives. These shifting definitions of the parameters of lifetime periods and perceived length of lifespans created challenges with aggregating information across individuals who did not share the same chronological age delimiters for phases of life. In our case, the use of life history matrices led to the development of a questionnaire (with structured questions) that asked participants to endorse a limited number of items that they engaged in during childhood (however they understood childhood) versus what they practiced at the time of interview (adults of various ages). In retrospect, this iteration of instrument development was also fraught with limitations. In the future, it should be noted that an ethnographer could delimit the life history matrix with chronological ages to address the issue described above.

Questionnaires

In the questionnaire that our team subsequently developed and administered (partial results were presented in chapter 3), we developed simple questions that asked participants to recall what they did as farmers during their childhood and what they currently do as farmers today. Then, results between general distal and proximal periods of the lifespan would be compared. Questionnaires are a useful way of obtaining data that provide a crude picture of how things might have radically changed over time in a farming community. Items on a questionnaire can sometimes feel abstract for participants, and they are prone to producing errors associated with self-

TABLE 4.1 Questionnaire items measuring life cycle changes in herbicide use

Spanish	English
¿Durante su niñez usaron herbicidas?	Did you use herbicides during your childhood?
□ Sí	□ Yes
□ No	□ No
¿Usa herbicida?	Do you currently use herbicides?
□ Sí	□ Yes
□ No	□ No

report. While a questionnaire designer may try to be as specific as possible by providing strict recall periods to a participant, this does not mean that the participant is going to readily remember and answer questions about a given recall period (e.g., exposure during the past week) that is abstractly referenced in the text of a questionnaire. For this study, we used general questions that were not specific to a predefined period. When asking the question in Spanish, we also used the implied subject pronoun "you all" when referring to practices experienced during childhood, since farmers were typically working with their family during that phase of life and usually were not the primary decision-makers about the chemicals being used on milpas during childhood. For example, the questions in table 4.1 illustrate how information might be obtained with a loose recall period that is open to interpretation.

For each of the questions above, numeric values are assigned to the response provided by the participant (Yes=1, No=0) and frequency distributions across all participants in the sample can be examined. While this style of interviewing and collecting data is not conducive to capturing context or information provided outside of the response set, and while it allows for variable concepts of "childhood" to be applied between participants, it does permit crude comparisons of changes within the individual's life cycle of what happened "then" versus "now." Across multiple individuals sampled in a community, this type of interview can also be used to understand broad changes in the use of agrichemicals over distal and varying points in time.

Results derived from questionnaires illustrate changes in the use of agrichemicals between childhood and current practice for 128 farmers who were interviewed using this type of questionnaire. Results are summarized in table 4.2. Across all 128 farmers, results illustrate appreciable increases over the lifespan in the use of herbicides (35% in childhood versus 97% in

TABLE 4.2 Personal life cycle changes in farming practice, childhood versus current, N = 128 farmers

Childhood versus current farming practices	N	Percent reporting practice
Tilled the soil during childhood	116	90.6
Tills the soil during adulthood	114	89.8
Used synthetic chemical fertilizers during childhood	54	42.2
Uses synthetic chemical fertilizers during adulthood	101	78.9
If so (n = 100), mixes ash into synthetic chemical fertilizers	17	17.0
Used herbicides during childhood	45	35.2
Uses herbicides during adulthood	121	96.8
Used pesticide to control plagues during childhood	64	50.0
Uses pesticide to control plagues during adulthood	121	94.5
Burned the land during childhood without herbicides	90	70.3
If burned, years they allowed land to rest		
Less than 2 years	37	41.6
2–3 years	35	39.3
3–4 years	10	11.2
More than 4 years	7	7.9
Burns the land during adulthood without herbicides	41	32.5
If burns land, do they burn all of the milpa or parts of it		
All	8	19.5
Parts	33	80.5
Used tabanco to store grain in childhood	74	58.3
Uses tabanco to store grain in adulthood	0	0.0

adulthood) and pesticides to address plagues (50% in childhood versus 95% in adulthood), and a reduction in the use of fire to control weeds (70% during childhood versus 33% in adulthood). Among those who used to burn the land to remove weeds, over 50% reported allowing the land to rest for at least two years after burning it. In some cases, this required coordination with other community members as sections of land were rotated and left for rest. Another appreciable finding is the eradication of the *tabanco*, which is an architectural structure designed for curing seeds by smoke. Farmers used to store corn seed above the house in a room that would cure the seed stores with smoke. The attic floor was lined with bamboo and salt leaves, and the smoke from the kitchen would seep through the floorboards and enter the attic where the corn was kept. The roof was made of *tejas* (clay tiles), which eventually allowed the smoke to escape. The smoke stayed inside the structure for a prolonged period and produced a constant heat in the space where the corn was stored, cured, and protected from weevils, ants, and other creatures that would threaten the food stores. While the tabanco could have posed other health hazards to humans (e.g., the inhalation of particulate matter, particularly for women responsible for working in the kitchens), the eradication of the tabanco corresponded to a shift in seed storage practices associated with the introduction of agrichemicals. When the data for this study were collected (2019), the common practice to store seeds was to use aluminum phosphide tablets in perforated tin cans placed underneath the grain mass in home silos. In our sample, 58% had a tabanco as a child, whereas no participants (0%) reported having a tabanco in adulthood. This last finding provides a pivotal point for understanding one of the drivers of increased individual reliance on agrichemicals throughout the community over such a short period of time.

Using the agrichemical recall inventory in the questionnaire data, we used random forest algorithms to identify factors associated with self-reported kidney issues. We identified an interaction between farmworker age, change in herbicide use over the life course, and the number of herbicides used. We found that self-reported kidney issues were elevated among older farmers who did not use herbicides during childhood but who began using multiple (3+) herbicides in their older age (Anastario et al. 2021b). The finding does not address causality but, rather, raises questions about the ways in which sequences of agrichemical exposures over the life course may correlate with self-reported kidney problems.

Life History Calendars

To be attentive to the complexity of plants that are encountered and maintained in a variety of contexts, Virginia Nazarea (2005, 19) suggests shifting some attention from aggregate units (organizations, populations) to the actual people who acquire and transmit knowledge individually, collectively, experimentally, and creatively. Documenting those individual stories, and analyzing them in such a way as to retain rich detail provided by multiple people, presents a methodological challenge that invites innovation and development. In this case, we are interested in the people who maintain intimate relationships with traditional corn, bean, and squash varieties. Both people and the plants associated with Chalateca milpa farming are now imbricated with agrichemicals that are not disappearing or going away but that have increasingly appeared over time in autobiographical memory. Individual people and individual agrichemicals can be analyzed and regrouped in certain ways that may not have been easy to see using preestablished categories, units, and methods for documenting people and the chemicals they interact with over time.

While conducting participant observation and interviews, stories involving agrichemicals were told with great attention to detail, particularly concerning ammonium sulphate (fertilizer), paraquat (herbicide), and cypermethrin (insecticide) used during particular periods of the lifespan. The specificity of the detail made it difficult to capture, let alone characterize, the detail that was being provided by different participants of different ages. Stories of starting, stopping, experimenting with, sleeping beside, accidentally ingesting, getting misted by, and inappropriately using specific agrichemicals over the lifespan had characteristics that could be explored quantitatively. The stories were reminiscent of the sociologist Georg Simmel's analytic focus on interactions that re-create social institutions, as opposed to beginning social analysis with an abstract idea of an institution that individuals fit into. Simmel's (1955, 172) assertion that "sociological patterns are revealed in social life in an unlimited number of ways" inspires a way to think about identifying patterns in human-chemical interactions across the lifespan of individuals who experienced similar (or divergent) things with specific nonhumans (agrichemicals) over the lifespan. In other words, groups of farmers may have used and been exposed to specific agrichemicals in particular sequences over their lifespans that are distinct from the sequences of use and exposure identified by other groups of farmers. The imperative of the farmworkers who told these detailed stories and posed urgent questions about their impacts to an outside researcher led us to focus on developing a method for capturing and analyzing these stories as they were told, but which could also potentially quantify patterns of use and exposure by chronological age of the farmer, which could subsequently be used to understand affiliation by synchronous experiences of agrichemical use over lifespans. The methodological development is ongoing, and its early stages are described here as they were inspired by this ethnographic work in El Salvador. Mike has since gone on to further develop these methods with foreign-born agricultural workers (from Central America and Mexico) living in the United States (Anastario et al. 2022a, 2022b), but these methodological developments are grounded in conducting participant observation with Salvadoran milpa farmers who anchor agrichemical recall to fertilizers that drive the corn growth cycle.

Life history calendars (LHCs) offer a balance between the life history matrix described by Nazarea and the need to capture quantifiable data that are often elicited in questionnaires. LHCs are thought to enhance retrospective reporting by reflecting the structure of autobiographical reporting (Belli 1998), establishing life periods and events before anchoring recall of event-specific knowledge. LHCs can appear in many forms, but they are usually structured as a grid-format timeline for collecting multiple domains of interest over a defined time period (see figure 4.2) (Freedman et al. 1988; Glasner and van der Vaart 2009). To better promote participant interaction and to encourage participants to correct interviewers, we print the matrices on 30" × 42" poster-sized sheets of paper and color-code responses such that participants who speak (but cannot read or write) Spanish can still visually follow the interview, anchor their responses to lines drawn in different colors across the page, and correct the interviewer or return to a previous response during the interview (Anastario et al. 2022b). This approach has its limits based on participants' visual abilities but provides one alternative for interviewing farmers with varying degrees of literacy. LHCs have been favored in public health research for their utility in aiding memory recollection when working with populations with low literacy levels, and/or with very complex and extensive work histories (Engel, Keifer, and Zahm 2001; Engel et al. 2001; Zahm et al. 2001). They have been particularly useful in measuring agrichemical exposures relative to periods of the life course where it would otherwise be difficult to conduct an assessment. For example, Quandt et al. (2020) used information collected via LHC as a proxy to determine pre- and postnatal exposure to pesticides in Latinx children from farmworker families in the United States. In Nicaragua, Rodríguez et al. (2012) used icon-calendar-based forms to interview parents about children's pre- and postnatal pesticide exposures to develop cumulative indices of exposure, identifying a total of forty-seven reported pesticides and concluding that a retrospective construction of cumulative pesticide-use indices could improve the assessment of quantitative exposure. A similar study in Costa Rica used an icon-calendar form to assess pesticide exposure during the perinatal period and found an elevated risk of childhood leukemia in association with parents' occupational exposures during the perinatal period and first year

FIGURE 4.2 Blank life history calendar.

of the child's life (Monge et al. 2007). While LHCs may show promise for improving recall of self-reported exposures, they must be tailored for the setting in which they are applied. As discussed earlier, farmers may anchor their recall of pesticides to fertilizers applied during the corn growth cycle, even though fertilizers themselves may not be of interest to researchers. Developing an instrument that could collect structured data while allowing for nonlinear ways of remembering and narrating human-chemical interactions remains a focal point for our ongoing development of LHCs. The idea is to capture experiences with human-chemical interactions over the lifespan of people who have experience with farming milpas.

The idea for developing a LHC to measure windows of the lifespan during which individual farmers were exposed to specific agrichemicals was informed directly by ethnographic research, but the methodology was not piloted until four years after recuperative observation began. The time it took to develop a quantitative instrument that grew from insights garnered through field notes represents an example of "slow research," and bears similarity to the slow processes of interdisciplinary knowledge production described by Elizabeth Roberts (2021) in her development of bioethnography. Sometimes, methodologies had to be implemented and data analyzed to inform the conclusion that a certain methodology (e.g., verbally administered questionnaires without visual cues) might not be the best method for eliciting recall of agrichemicals during earlier periods of the lifespan among milpa farmers of different ages. Mike later piloted LHCs with agricultural workers in South Florida who migrated from Central America and Mexico, many of whom farmed milpas before engaging in agricultural wage labor in the United States (Anastario et al. 2022a). Among twenty-two participants in that study who were in the same age group as those who would be at risk for CKDu (eighteen to forty-five years), the LHC was useful in showing how the greatest person-years of self-reported exposure to several agrichemicals occurred prior to international migration (while participants were still living in Central America) for the now-adult agricultural workers (see figure 4.3).

The greatest person-years of self-reported exposure to numerous agrichemicals generally occurred in the eleven-to-fifteen-year age range. This period was notably associated with the greatest person-years of exposure to parathion and paraquat, two particularly toxic agrichemicals. Being able to

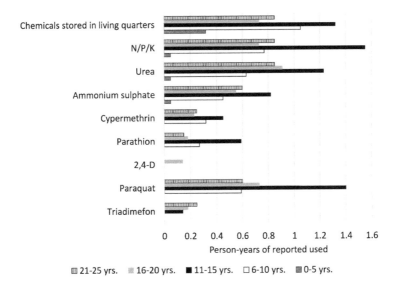

FIGURE 4.3 LHC-derived agrichemical use relative to age of self-reported exposure among workers of Mesoamerican descent living in South Florida, *n* = 22.

identify patterns such as these in farmers' stories of agrichemical use and exposure may be helpful in articulating how sequences of exposure across the lifespan may be implicated in diseases observed later in life. In this study, it is also possible to see how fertilizers that drive the corn growth cycle (N/P/K, ammonium sulphate, and urea) are remembered and may assist researchers with understanding farmers' exposomes by offering better mnemonic anchors for farmers during the interview process.

LHCs can be further analyzed with the use of social sequence analysis (a quantitative technique not described here) that may help to elucidate affinity typologies between actors who may not share physical interactions, but share experiences that emerge through synchronous acts (Cornwell 2015). Social sequence analysis can be useful, for example, in characterizing classes and patterns of agrichemical exposures across milpa farmers. This highly structured approach to capturing human-chemical interactions across the lifespan privileges the stories of farmers who narrate specific exposures as they wonder whether these past exposures play a role in today's illnesses. The LHCs are one quantitative way to harness important findings informed by field notes and provide avenues for farmers to remember early life exposures by establishing context and facilitating moments for the interviewee to see the data that are being collected from them.

Conclusion

This study of more-than-human intimacies was littered with inorganic, nonhuman actants that appeared and reappeared in the lifeways and recollections of Chalateco milpa farmers. The imperative to adapt and further develop methods that document, analyze, and inform an understanding of the presence of these nonhumans in the life stories of farmers stemmed directly from an ethical imperative to take seriously farmers' concerns about the agrichemicals they used and asked outside observers about. We showed how participant observation can be informative to the development of instruments that result in quantified representations of human-chemical interactions for the purpose of retrospective exposure assessment.

By building upon and drawing from methods for eliciting agrarian life and community histories (Nazarea 1998, 2005) and Elizabeth Roberts' (2021) development of bioethnography, we illustrated a sequence of methods that began with participant observation and ended with life history calendars that could assist researchers with the quantitative reconstruction of exposure histories. The reconstruction of exposure histories, informative to an understanding of milpa farmers' exposomes, is methodologically grounded in ethnography. Documenting farmers' questions about agrichemicals, the everyday ways in which farmers encounter them, and the fertilizers that help them recall exposures are some of the ways in which ethnography holds incredible potential, not only for reconstructing exposures but for methodologically recuperating how farmers remember hazardous chemicals that have appeared in their everyday environments over their individual lifespans.

FIVE
Vicarious Intimacy and Contemporary Art

Synopsis

In this chapter, we examine how more-than-human intimacies travel away from assemblages through human networks and rematerialize in contemporary art, returning human attention back to nonhumans that assemble with humans in processes of vicarious intimacy. This chapter explores different forms of contemporary Salvadoran art that not only lend to an analysis of vicarious intimacy but help us imagine numerous processes of vicarious intimacies that occur relative to more-than-human assemblages. We consider two "sets" of art in this chapter. The first set explores the work of artists who directly address botanical matter derived from Salvadoran milpas. The second set considers processes of vicarious intimacy concerning nonhuman actants in more-than-human assemblages beyond the parameters of milpa farming but within the context of El Salvador. We are inspired to think with contemporary Salvadoran artists to imagine vicarious intimacies that are derived from and constituents of more-than-human assemblages.

Vicarious Intimacy and Visual Art

The movement of more-than-human intimacies away from milpa farming through human networks is something we refer to as "vicarious intimacy." Vicarious intimacy is both a process and type of more-than-human intimacy that arises in the more-than-human assemblages, in this case transmitted to and among people who remember milpas, their family members' memories of farming milpas, or, more abstractly, intimacies imbricated with nonhuman actants in more-than-human assemblages. We consider that intimacies formed in more-than-human assemblages may "depart" and travel outward, simultaneously reattuning peoples' attention back to the more-than-human assemblages they emanate from. These intimacies can emerge in affective processes of nostalgia, recuperation, imagination, and endearment. Sometimes the plant matter produced on Salvadoran milpas travels far away from the place where the seeds were sown and the plants were grown. It gets nixtamalized and converted into *masa* (dough) before being clapped into tortillas in rural home kitchens and urban markets where workers get lunch and dogs roam the hallways. People who eat the tortillas may engage in everyday conversation about the milpa or milpas from which the corn was derived and the varieties of corn that were planted, or may even talk about their longing for varieties that are considered lost. This would be an example of a process of vicarious intimacy connected to gastronomy (the everyday art of making tortillas) that will be discussed further in chapter 6. While we conceive of vicarious intimacy in relation to milpa farming, contemporary Salvadoran artists inspire us to imagine the possibilities of that intimacy in other more-than-human assemblages beyond milpa farming (see figure 5.1). To think with vicarious intimacies and their possibilities, we offer the metaphor of an electron orbiting the nucleus of an atom. The electron (intimacy) travels far and unpredictable distances away from the nucleus while also playing a role in developing bonds, compounds, and molecules that might affect what the atom is or becomes. In this chapter and the next, we consider the ways in which vicarious intimacies may play a role in materializations and processes of more-than-human assemblages.

Contemporary art is one way in which vicarious intimacies with botanical matter may materialize. In her ethnographic research and aesthetic approach to Ethiopian *ensete* (a root crop in the banana family), Valentina Peveri (2020, 206–8) finds parallels in her research practice with contemporary Ethiopian artist Elizabeth Wold, who worked with ensete as a medium. Experimenting with the plant through different media, for both ethnographer and artist, were approaches that Peveri (2020, 206–8) characterized as a "radical departure." Peveri's notion of radical departures inspires our analysis of vicarious intimacies that move through humans imbricated with nonhumans in more-than-human assemblages and that may materialize or be transmitted through the material of contemporary art.

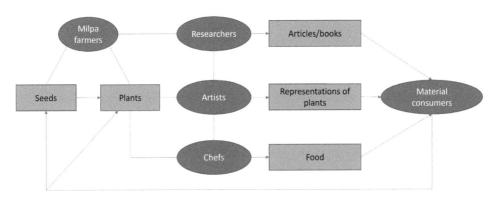

FIGURE 5.1 Pathways of more-than-human intimacy in the more-than-human assemblages of the milpa.

In this chapter, we review four types of contemporary Salvadoran art that affectively attune viewer/reader attention back to the milpa, or nonhumans and humans in more-than-human assemblages. We organize the art examined into two "sets" of contemporary Salvadoran art. The first set grounds processes of vicarious intimacy derived from the Salvadoran milpa in contemporary art forms and includes embroidery produced by Salvadoran refugees during the civil war and art representing plant-human relations produced by Wilber Salguero, an artist whose family is from the region of Chalatenango where a large portion of the ethnographic research presented in this book was conducted. The second set of art illustrates vicarious intimacy in more-than-human assemblages that are not milpa farming, and which help us imagine the possibilities and forms that vicarious intimacy may assume in more-than-human assemblages. The second set of art includes the work of Muriel Hasbun, particularly regarding her integration of remembered botanical material in art, and engravings by Efraín Caravantes that directly invite viewers to reflect on processes of producing art that implicates intimacies shared in human networks concerning nonhuman actants.

To select the contemporary art depicted in this chapter, we did not begin with a centralized repository or clearly defined parameters of the universe of contemporary Salvadoran art. Rather, we worked through our own networks to identify art made by artists who were either living today, or could be living today, and with whom we could also speak (to the best of our ability) about some of the intimacies with which the art is concerned. We present the work of artists who we could directly access (and seek permissions from), or collectors (such as museums) that were fostering not only the collection but the ongoingness of an art form (embroidery). Terry Smith (2019, 1) describes contemporary art as "pervasively, an art to come" that harbors historical longing, repetitions, and recursions to the past and to earlier art forms. Smith (2019, 223) identifies a tendency within the contemporary art world to seek another "temporal inhabitation" that escapes the present. What is common to each of the works presented in this chapter is that they invite the viewer to share in an intimacy while turning the viewer's gaze backward to nonhuman actants that were intimately assembled with people. In this way, the contemporary art we discuss can be thought of as illustrating vicarious intimacies and its possibilities within and beyond milpa farming.

To account for the passage of time and what is remembered/represented in the art, we build from the concept of restorative nostalgia (emphasizing the Greek *nostos*, the "return home," where there is an attempt to restore the past in the present) that inspired much of the foundational research for this book (Anastario 2019, 56; Boym 2001). Instead of viewing the act of the artist materializing something of the remembered past as restorative, we employ the concept of "re-membering" to refer to the material depiction that partially recuperates elements of more-than-human assemblages of the past (botanical material, nonhuman actants) in the material art of the present. We build from Karen Barad's (2017) description of re-membering to account for the "material reconfiguring of spacetimemattering" that not only acknowledges the ruin of the past, but also produces new openings and histories. While our analysis in this chapter is somewhat brief and superficial with regard to the body of work produced by each artist, working with these concepts invites attention to each artists' method. In some cases, the artist explicitly asks the viewer to focus on method (Caravantes). In others, the viewer is confronted with botanical matter (Hasbun), representations of botanical matter entwined with family memory (Salguero), or botanical matter that was laboriously represented but easy to miss (war-themed embroideries). Each artist re-members something nonhuman in the materialized art, and in doing so processes vicarious intimacies derived from and constitutive of more-than-human assemblages.

Embroidery Among Salvadorans During Wartime and Protracted Postwar Periods

Embroideries produced during and after the Salvadoran Civil War depict components of the milpa that are re-membered with representations of wartime conflict. Some of the embroideries were generated in exile, while others were generated in workshops long after the conflict. Some of the embroideries can be viewed as historical documents that circulated during the war and across borders. They have been recuperated in the form of collections (museums and exhibitions) and have inspired workshops (for current embroiderers and embroiderers to come). While much attention is given to the depictions of wartime violence in the embroidered cloths, the nonhuman elements therein illustrate processes of vicarious intimacy that return the embroiderer's attention, viewer's attention, and reader's attention back to the landscape and milpas from which the refugees fled.

Below, we discuss embroideries that were made by Salvadoran women in refugee camps in the border regions of Honduras between 1980 and 1989, or that were generated in more recent workshops that facilitate processes of remembering and embroidering. While the population of embroideries generated during wartime and postwar periods is not accessible in a single repository, a substantial number of them have been collected by the *Museo de la Palabra y la Imagen* (Museum of the Word and the Image of El Salvador [MUPI]), whose digital image bank has been made available for viewing through the University of Texas at Austin (MUPI 2009). Our analysis is derived from an examination of thirty-two pieces and focused on embroideries that depict landscapes and milpas.

In daily life, Salvadoran women in the countryside traditionally embroidered everyday items such as tablecloths, cloth used for keeping corn tortillas, *cuturinas* (small and delicate infant garments), and handkerchiefs that could be used for waving breeze onto infants in a crowded bus (Silber 2022). While there are multiple origin stories of the embroideries that have come to depict Salvadoran wartime violence, they would eventually be created for international audiences and contribute to calls for international solidarity (Todd 2021a, 41–42). The art form and political context of the embroideries bears similarities with the *arpillera* (patchwork) art made by Chilean women during the Pinochet era, where found fabrics were used to create depictions of resistance, human rights violations, and poverty during the 1970s and 1980s (Bryan-Wilson 2017, 149). Many of the Salvadoran embroideries were created in foreign camps formed by the United Nations Refugee Agency Fund (UNHCR) that received hundreds of displaced people during the Salvadoran Civil War (1979–92). Some of the embroideries that we show here are from refugees in the camps of Mesa Grande, Colomoncagua, and La Virtud. Recently, the MUPI began a project of investigating and collecting embroideries created by refugee women in La Virtud and Mesa Grande who had originated from the Department of Chalatenango. This was made possible through a project that was headquartered in Las Vueltas, Chalatenango. These daylong events were designed to incorporate younger generations of the community. The MUPI aims to collect the results of the recent workshop and create an exhibition focused on Chalateca's memories of exile. From 2017 onward, a series of exhibits and collections has highlighted these embroideries. While the physical origin, year of generation, and embroiderer are unknown to the authors in most of the cases (despite our best attempts to collect this information), the milpa re-membered through the embroideries that circulate in these workshops and collections are of interest to our analysis.

Below, we present two embroideries that were from the civil war period (figures 5.2 and 5.3), one which may have been generated during the war, but whose date of origin is more questionable given the condition and color of the fabric and thread (figure 5.4), and one which is almost certainly from a later, postwar era (figure 5.5) as indicated by the conditions of fabric and thread (Molly Todd, pers. comm., May 25, 2023). In each of the embroideries pictured in the figures, representations of wartime violence are overarching and salient. However, the discursive focus on war that has emerged surrounding the embroideries eschews the intimate attention to milpas that are re-membered in these fabrics (most of which were *manta, cuadrillé* or *serenata*): a memory of plants in a landscape enveloped by a traumatic process of displacement. The embroiderers also re-member *bodegones* (fruits and foodstuffs) and forested landscapes, composed of trees and shrubs, milpas, crops, orchards, gardens, flowers and birds. Women re-membered the milpa through embroidered fabrics that provide testimonies of wartime conflict, documenting agrarian lifeways that preexisted physical displacement, and that were important enough to dedicate attention to when creating a depiction of war. However, the women's displacement did not signify total detachment, as the displaced Salvadorans "continued to mobilize and act with an eye toward a better future" (Todd 2021a, 24–25), and the embroideries could very well reflect that prospective gaze.

The shared past, shared space, and natural elements of the landscape are interpreted in a unique way by each one of the embroiderers, in whose work no tree, flower, plant, shrub, or vegetable is the same and yet certain specific plants can be identified: papaya and morro trees; agaves; *flores de Pascua*

FIGURE 5.2 Embroidery, Colomoncagua Refugees, We Want Peace. Photo courtesy of the Museum of the Word and the Image of El Salvador.

FIGURE 5.3 Embroidery, Mesa Grande, We Fled So Not to Die Because of Bombs, Leaving Our Little Houses Abandoned. Photo courtesy of the Museum of the Word and the Image of El Salvador.

(poinsettias), *pasiflora* (passionflower), *lirios* (lilies), *jacintos* (hyacinths), *campanillas* (bluebells), and *claveles* (carnations); fruits such as apples, pineapples, mangos, and grapes; vegetables like radishes, beets, red onions, carrots, lettuce, and corn; and, of course, the milpa. The milpa (or plants derived from it) appears in the landscape beside a house or on the patio of a family home much like Chepe's milpita that was described in the Introduction of this book. Victoria Sanford (2003, 143) illustrated how, in Guatemala, natural elements of the landscape can form a "living memory of terror" in

FIGURE 5.4 Embroidery, Santa Marta Community, Peasant Working the Land, The Mother Cooking the Foods, Women's Group. Photo courtesy of the Museum of the Word and the Image of El Salvador.

individual and collective memories of rural Mayans. The Salvadoran embroideries transmit images of wartime terror. Milpas are depicted alongside roads where vehicles are traveling (figure 5.2), underneath scenes foreshadowing aerial bombardment (figure 5.4), or beside a rebel fighter (figure 5.5). In figure 5.3, the mountainous land where milpas would be cultivated burns as refugees flee from town, the branch of a tree falling in the distance.

In the embroideries, milpas are re-membered by women who embroidered outside of, yet simultaneously within, the domestic sphere. Displaced by political violence and in some cases producing the embroideries for an international audience, the embroiderers are doing something that contains subversive elements (Vinebaum 2020) while simultaneously reinforcing traditional gender norms. Women are depicted as cooking (figures 5.2 and 5.4)

FIGURE 5.5 Embroidery, Estela Radista (Radio Operator). Photo courtesy of the Museum of the Word and the Image of El Salvador.

and carrying children (figure 5.3) and are not generally depicted as laboring in the fields. However, newer embroidery (produced after the war) depicts a woman guerilla fighter (figure 5.5). At the same time, women are the those who re-membered the milpa through the embroideries, simultaneously reinforcing a trope of rural male agricultural laborers (showing farming in figure 5.4). Thread, needle, and cloth are used to materialize a testimony of the lived experienced of conflict and to remember an image of a past place, the final product bearing no particular form of everyday use other than to tell a highly significant story for multiple audiences who are paying attention to them. In several of the more recent postwar workshops, young boys have been taught how to embroider. The finished products both flex against and buttress traditional gender norms as rural pasts are retold and re-membered through embroidery.

The visual re-membering of the original landscape is reminiscent of the Chilean arpilleras, where seeds, sticks, grains, and other nonhuman objects were embedded within the textiles (Bryan-Wilson 2017, 157). While the Salvadoran embroideries represent nonhumans with thread, they do so in a way that reimagines a location that the embroiderer can inhabit while embroidering out-of-place, from afar. Working to embroider the past in the present regarding a subject matter that is interlaced with corn, crops, and other plants is how environmental re-membering materializes. The re-membering recuperates a more-than-human intimacy with the milpa amid the material representation of a wartime testimony. It potentially transmits a range of traumatic and aesthetic elements as sense is made of the past in the present. The symmetrical attention to elements of the milpa amid wartime violence provides images that viewers must consider long after the art has been produced. Understanding the embroideries discussed here as intimate renderings of a past-place, we see elements of the milpa appear and reappear through processes of vicarious intimacy, which is more-than-human intimacy that has traveled away from the milpa through human networks connected to it.

As a way of transitioning to the next artist considered in this first set of art that directly concerns the Salvadoran milpa, we highlight the embroidery depicting "Estela Radista" (figure 5.5). The embroidery illustrates a single woman dressed in guerrilla uniform standing beside a single stalk of corn. Unlike the wartime embroideries that emphasize collective experiences, the embroidery has only two key figures: a single woman (without community) and corn. The work of *radistas* (women radio operators) allowed many women to participate in operational work within the guerrilla without being confined to the kitchens and hospitals in the guerrilla camps. What is depicted could be argued as reflecting the intimate wartime and postwar-time entanglements of gender, conflict, and rural space (Silber 2010). This postwar creation of the individual, feminized agent beside an individual corn stalk transitions into the work of Wilber Salguero, an artist who is a descendent of a Chalateca agrarian family and who re-members elements of the milpa not beside but within and encapsulating the human figures depicted in his work.

Rural Postmemory in the Art of Wilber Salguero

The transmission of rural memories of the Chalateca milpa appears and re-appears in the art of Wilber Salguero (b. 1993), a designer and visual artist from El Salvador. The study of memory and its transmission, especially in El Salvador and Latin America, has tended to center on the transmission of a traumatic event from generation to generation. Sometimes these acts of memory transmission contribute toward the pursuit of justice, as is clearly illustrated in the embroideries. Salguero's familial memories of the Salvadoran milpa, transmitted to him during childhood and reinforced by his visits to and connections with Chalatenango growing up, appear within representations of agrarian bodies developed by the artist today.

Salguero is the descendent of a Chalateca agrarian family that transmitted memories of their agrarian past to him, informing what Salguero remembers, imagines, and ultimately renders into art. This can be observed in his works, including *Hombre de maíz* (Man of corn, 2020); *Hombre de café* (Man of coffee, 2021); *Lilies* (2022); *I saw that man in my garden . . .* (2022); *Va-ya-la-pa-pa-ya* (2020); and other illustrations of the milpa and corn that he has created since 2020.

These visual works, particularly those depicted in the Corn Man series, articulate what Salguero has personally described as "visual studies of the landscapes from my infancy and nostalgia. I grew up in San Salvador and Chalatenango (Dulce Nombre de Maria) and thinking about corn is remembering stories about the milpa that my father used to tell me, the atoles and trips that we used to make to the corn festival, and the food that feeds us and that fed our ancestors" (Salguero 2022, 2). In Salguero's art, the countryside and the milpa is reconstructed through the nostalgic memories of the family, subverting its traumatic origin and offering new possibilities of artistic representations that trouble traditional gendered representations of Salvadoran farmworkers. Salguero has no work experience on the milpa. The memory he draws from is one that is passed on by family members through storytelling, which resurfaces in Salguero's art in what might be considered a type of postmemory (Hirsch 2012). The Salguero Valdez family lived in Chalatenango until 1980, when they moved to Honduras at the start of the Salvadoran Civil War. In 1983, the family returned to El Salvador, but this time to the capital, San Salvador. Memories of the Salvadoran milpa were transmitted to Salguero who began to imagine and materially render non-

FIGURE 5.6 Wilber Salguero, *Hombre de maíz*, 2020. Image courtesy of artist.

violent depictions of humans entangled with botanical elements, many of which are derived from milpas. Unlike the wartime embroideries generated in exile, war does not appear in Salguero's art as an element that disrupts the landscape. Instead, Salguero "recuperates" elements of the landscape (Salamanca 2015), in which the postwar visual art mediates the landscape recreated as a primitive agrarian space untouched by violence—a landscape which the population could no longer see due to the war, especially in the mountainous region between Chalatenango and Morazán.

Traditionally, Salvadoran painting has represented a landscape without actors. The work of well-known Salvadoran painters including Pedro Ángel

FIGURE 5.7 Wilber Salguero, *Hombre de café*, 2021. Image courtesy of artist.

Espinoza (1891–1939) and Miguel Ortiz Villacorta (1887–1963) illustrate the landscape as a crossroads between romanticism and custom, in which men are fieldworkers who confine themselves to their work as peons of the plantation, rarely turning their gaze outward toward the spectator, unlike the artists' portraits of politicians or aristocrats (Salamanca 2017). Both painters of the Salvadoran landscape, part of the nationalist movement between 1920 and 1940, pay more attention to nature than to the fieldworkers themselves as subjects with their own histories and identities. The paintings of Camilo Minero—a muralist who depicted the daily lives of agrarian workers in rural environments, and who lived in exile during the civil war until the signing of the Chapultepec Peace Accords (Reber 1978; Heidenry 2014)—reflect scenes of rural towns, milpas, and farmers that are still visible today. More recently, Wilber Salguero depicts an image in which the masculinity and/or

FIGURE 5.8 Wilber Salguero, *Lilies*, 2022. Image courtesy of artist.

boundaries of the farmworker's body can be contrasted with a patriarchal ideal (Connell 2003). In this sense, Salguero's rural figures (*Hombre de maíz* and *Hombre de café* in figures 5.6 and 5.7) embody stylized forms composed of plant matter that could be read as fragile and inhuman, illustrating the fruit of one's labor and the leaves of the plant, both comprising the laboring human. The Corn Man series depicts fluid bodies with questionable boundaries composed of botanical elements in Salguero's postmemory. More-than-human intimacies form between plants and people, and travel away

FIGURE 5.9 Wilber Salguero, *I saw that man in my garden . . .* ,
2022. Image courtesy of artist.

from the milpa in networks of humans through vicarious intimacy. Salguero's paintings both reflect the vicarious intimacy of the milpa experienced
within his family and transmit that vicarious intimacy to the viewer who
considers humans comprised of or entwined with botanical elements.

Depicting agrarian bodies in intimate relations with plants is emphasized
by the gender-fluid figures depicted in *Lilies* (2022), *I saw that man in my
garden . . .* (2022), and *Va-ya-la-pa-pa-ya* (2020) (figures 5.8–5.10), which
break traditional representations of masculinity among men interacting
with/working with plants. These works depict men unencumbered by masculine features and in intimate contact with botanical actants, including the

FIGURE 5.10 Wilber Salguero, *Va-ya-la-pa-pa-ya*, 2020. Image courtesy of artist.

flowers and fruits that they extract from the milpa or gardens, combining masculine and feminine elements that would typically be opposed in more classical renderings of rural life. Salguero feminizes rural men in his depictions of them by illustrating flowers, painted nails, and the act of carrying vegetable products for sale on the head. His work illustrates a tender and porous side of men in relation to plants. The more traditional male figures lack set boundaries that distinguish outside from inside, showing not only how plants get inside but rather compose the worker who cultivates them. Salguero's art depicts men attuned to, created from, and adorned by botanical matter. Salguero's representations depict men's intimate relations with plants and transmit an intimacy to the viewer that reattunes the viewer's attention to the milpa and botanical matter.

The art of Wilber Salguero and the embroideries both illustrate elements of the Salvadoran milpa within the art that the viewer/reader consumes. In this way, a type of everyday intimacy derived from peoples' contact with the milpa—be it the artist or someone related to the artist—reappears and is intimately shared between humans, reattuning and reorienting human attention back to the Salvadoran milpa in some way. This is a process of vicarious intimacy materialized in contemporary art through the process of re-membering the milpa. The next set of contemporary Salvadoran art includes the work of Muriel Hasbun, Verónica Vides, and Efraín Caravantes. The art illustrates vicarious intimacy by re-membering nonhuman actants from more-than-human assemblages of the past.

Muriel Hasbun

Muriel Hasbun is a Salvadoran American educator and artist whose work is focused on issues of migration, memory, postmemory, and cultural identity. Hasbun (2016) describes herself as having "an extreme sensitivity to the irreconcilable." Born in El Salvador to a family that was devastated by the Holocaust, Hasbun grew up in a diasporic space until she herself migrated to the United States during the violence of the Salvadoran Civil War (Oslé 2022). In her art, Hasbun explores her family history and sense of identity through documents, photos, oral histories, and the reconstruction of her own perceptions. Hasbun's photo-based work has been internationally exhibited, and her composite memorial images have contributed to sharpened analyses of the "postmemorial photographic aesthetic and the psychic structures that motivate it" (Hirsch and Spitzer 2006). Here we focus on a recurring actant that appears in both material and representational forms in Hasbun's art: fallen thorns from *vachellia cornigera* (bullhorn acacia tree), which Hasbun refers to as ixcanal thorns in her work (*ixcanal* is the Quiché Mayan word used to refer to the thorny trees) (Taube 1989).

Acacias are one of the largest genera of shrubs and trees on the planet. They make polysaccharide gums that help seal wounds to discourage opportunistic bacteria and fungi, they fix nitrogen, and they protect themselves from predators with thorns and symbiotic ant colonies that flourish within their thorns (Haraway 2016, 122–23). Thinking about vachellia cornigera inspires thinking with and about assemblages. In El Salvador, the thorns fall from the trees and can be found on hillslopes, riverbeds, and beaches. As a child, Hasbun would encounter and collect these thorns, returning to collect them and incorporating both physical and representational forms of the fallen thorns in artistic renderings of a re-membered past. In *Protegida / Watched Over*, which premiered at the fiftieth Venice Biennale in 2003 and was then shown at the Corcoran Gallery of Art in 2004 in a solo show entitled *Memento: Muriel Hasbun Photographs*, the installation included a triptych that had ixcanal thorns from El Salvador woven onto fabric set upon wood constructions (figure 5.11).

The plant matter is re-membered within the artwork, physically appearing for the viewer to ponder. This style of re-membering is reminiscent of the Chilean arpilleras discussed earlier where seeds, sticks, grains, and other

FIGURE 5.11 Muriel Hasbun, *Ave Maria, Triptych III*, from the series *Protegida / Watched Over*, dorso panels, gelatin silver prints (on recto), ixcanal thorns, fabric, wood constructions, 2003. Image courtesy of artist.

nonhuman objects were embedded within the textiles (Bryan-Wilson 2017, 157). In the context of Hasbun's art, the ixcanal thorns draw the viewer/ reader's attention directly to plant matter that plays a critical role in the plant's protection, and the onto-epistemological quest of the artist-as-child to protect her family. It conjures intimate images of the artist's past, while bringing the viewer face to face with material that transmits human intimacy through attunement to botanical matter in El Salvador. Thorns are also a Christian symbol associated with suffering in Western art and allude to the Catholic church protecting Hasbun's mother by hiding her (and coopting her Jewishness and how she saw herself). In this case, the botanical matter is not derived from the milpa, although acacia trees do sometimes speckle the sides of mountains where milpas grow. Hasbun re-members botanical elements from her experience, facilitating a process of vicarious intimacy with the viewer/reader who considers the botanical material and the role that it played in the complex milieu of the artist's experience of landscape, intergeneration trauma, postmemory, and diaspora.

Re-Turning the Nonhuman in the Human: The Art of Efraín Caravantes and Verónica Vides

In a manner similar to the methodological practice of recuperative observation described in chapter 2, Efraín Caravantes at times aims to lose control of the (artistic) intervention, introducing randomness into the artistic production process in such a way that the viewer is forced to confront and consider the artist's method. An intimacy of the artist is transmitted through re-membered elements of the artist's more-than-human past, potentially leaving the viewer/reader feeling startled, unsettled, and/or contemplating how the material was produced as intimacy is transmitted both within the work and to the viewer/reader.

We provide context for the specific series by Caravantes discussed here by first providing context for how the series appeared in El Salvador relative to the art of Verónica Vides (El Salvador, 1970). Both Caravantes' and Vides' work appeared together in San Salvador at the fourth *Fiesta Ecléctica de las Artes* (Eclectic Festival of the Arts [FEA]) in 2015. Vides produced seeds that were abstract and constructed, located alongside a clay image of a woman staring at her own genitals. Vides' first "seeds" were part of a study of the repetition of certain figures in beings or organisms. Vides had experimented with the production of archetypes of women excluded from the patriarchal mandate of femininity, echoing the "Madwomen" series of poems by the Chilean poet Gabriela Mistral (2008). During a period in which Vides began working with organic materials, she moved from San Salvador to the mountains of Chalatenango, where she founded her studio in her family's home. Vides eventually began producing sculptures of bald women from fired clay, where the women are naked, with the skin stuck to the bone, exposing, showing, or looking at their own vulvas (1999–2001). At the 2015 FEA exhibit, Vides reexhibited one of these clay madwomen: *Loca* (Crazy, ca. 1999). *Loca* showed her vulva. Beside her, on a bed of gravel, some ceramic seeds were placed in a sculptural installation. The seeds were shaped like husks. In effect, they resembled open vulvas (figure 5.12). Vides' seed vulvas were in the exposition leading into the room where the *Semen. Los moldes del azar* (Semen. Molds by chance) series by Efraín Caravantes was exhibited. Together, the work of Vides and Caravantes can also be considered a play on the concept of open pollination that is dealt with by this book's focus on in-situ conservation in Chalatenango.

FIGURE 5.12 Verónica Vides, *Loca* (Crazy, ca. 1999), presented at FEA in 2015. Photograph by Efraín Caravantes.

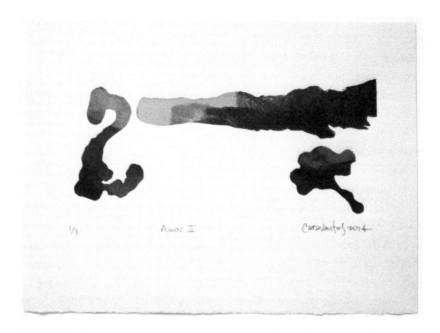

FIGURE 5.13 Efraín Caravantes, *Amor II*, from the series *Semen. Los moldes del azar*, 2014. Image courtesy of artist.

In *Semen. Los moldes del azar*, engravings of human semen are exhibited. In 2012, Caravantes asked eight participants (friends and artists in his own network) to ejaculate on linoleum. Caravantes himself was the ninth participant. After drying, the semen prints generated unique figures created through random movement that could not be subject to the control of the artist (see figure 5.13). The fluid was then traced by the participants and subsequently cut out by Caravantes to create engraving molds. For four years, Caravantes worked with and created engravings from the shared molds derived from his network of friends, which has changed over the years. The entire series, titled *Semen. Los moldes del azar*, was shown in 2015, during FEA. Caravantes explicitly sought to generate art from something momentary, unused, and that moved in random patterns, and he would have to integrate the outcome into what has traditionally been a repetitive, standardized process. In doing so, Caravantes experimentally interrupted the process of production and asks viewers/readers to contemplate the method behind what is being represented. The case of Caravantes' series inverts our focus on more-than-human assemblages that produce more-than-human intimacies

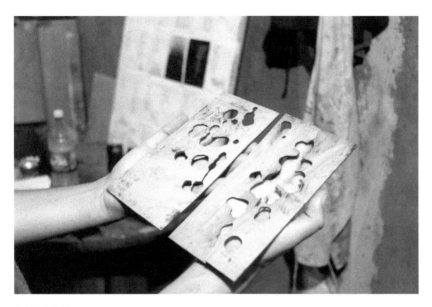

FIGURE 5.14 Efraín Caravantes, holding linoleum from the series *Semen. Los moldes del azar*, remembering the names and people associated with linoleum from eight years prior, 2022.

that travel away from the assemblage through people. Caravantes created a more-than-human assemblage predicated on intimacies between people, and subsequently generated aesthetic images from the material remains of the assemblage in the absence of those people that he now remembers (figure 5.14). His work speaks to Jane Bennett's assertion that we must

> admit that humans have crawled or secreted themselves into every corner of the environment; admit that the environment is actually inside human bodies and minds, and then proceed politically, technologically, scientifically, in everyday life, with careful forbearance, as you might with unruly relatives to whom you are inextricably bound and with whom you will engage over a lifetime, like it or not. Give up the futile attempt to disentangle the human from the nonhuman. (2010, 116)

The method used by Caravantes might provoke startlement or disgust, but those affective processes are entwined with unapologetic intimacy that reattune the viewer's attention back to the nonhuman actants that reassemble human connections in the artist's past. Amid what may be a simultaneously unsettling and aesthetically pleasing experience, intimacy is transmitted to the viewer in the physical absence of those friends who are re-membered through pieces of linoleum, remnants of a more-than-human assemblage of the past.

In the last fifteen years, Caravantes has been carrying out his own "archaeology," an archaeology of himself, working with the materials derived from his body, including fingernail clippings and electrocardiograms. The use of these materials is understood to be part of the artist's biography, having been part of his body at some point. *Espejo* is Caravantes' most recent work at the time this book is being written (figure 5.15). It consists of his own form traced on paper through the repetition of the engraved words "ego" and "echo" (*eco* in Spanish), creating a type of visual poetry. The particularity of the engraving is in the instrument used to generate it. Caravantes created his own engraving molds, one for each word, in the style of pre-Hispanic seals: modeled from clay then fired. Moreover, *Espejo* was finished with a red ink, a principal and sacred color in the temples of Indigenous cities such as Copán (Mayan) and Teotihuacán (Mexica). This is a historic exercise seeking to recuperate and regenerate lost techniques that have survived through oral transmissions and bibliographic references but not in practice; that is to say, the technique is not currently used. This methodological search implies rupture with historic continuity. Like the parallels that Peveri (2020, 206–8) draws between her research practice with contemporary Ethiopian artist Elizabeth Wold, we find parallels between the practice of recuperative observation (chapter 2) and Caravantes' partial recuperation of an old technique in the present. It simultaneously evokes an intimacy by re-membering nonhuman actants entangled with the human in more-than-human assemblages generated by the artist, transmitting an intimacy to the reader/viewer that reattunes attention back to the assemblage from which it emerged.

Conclusion

Vicarious intimacies are more-than-human intimacies that travel away from more-than-human assemblages by networks of people. In this chapter, we imagined how those intimacies are both represented and processed through materializations of contemporary art. We used the concept of "re-membering" to refer to the material depiction that partially recuperates el-

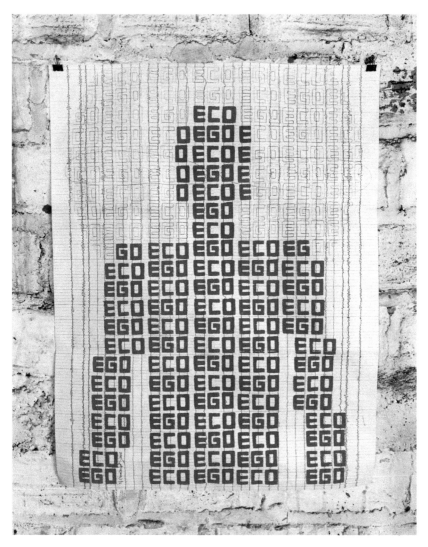

FIGURE 5.15 Efraín Caravantes, *Espejo*, 33″ × 26″, 2022. Image courtesy of artist.

ements of more-than-human assemblages of the past (botanical material, nonhuman actants) in the material art of the present, and which plays a role in re-attuning viewer/reader attention back to nonhuman elements of more-than-human assemblages. We find various similarities between themes explored in the world of contemporary Salvadoran art and the methods we used to examine more-than-human intimacies on the milpa, and are inspired by contemporary artists to imagine the possibilities of vicarious intimacy relative to and beyond the more-than-human assemblage of milpa farming.

In our analysis of the embroideries, we highlighted the secondary (or less obvious) themes of plants that appeared in environmental re-membering through embroideries that document wartime violence, particularly plants associated with the Salvadoran milpa. As research on collective memory among refugees and the regions from which they fled often focuses on the wartime period, wartime violence has arguably become a topic that precedes the people and the region itself. Here, we highlight the presence of plants that reference an integral and often overlooked agrarian lifeway that is being re-membered by the embroiderers. In a similar light, Muriel Hasbun incorporates collected botanical elements directly into her art as she processes a complex past in an intergenerational recounting of her family's story of genocide and persecution, intergenerational trauma, and, in her case, post-memory, all in the context of El Salvador's civil war. Hasbun re-members botanical actants that are entwined with the transmission of this intimacy to the viewer/reader. We emphasize the environmental re-membering evident in the embroidered Chalateca women's cloths and the fabric of Hasbun's triptych, where botanical materials are re-membered in art that evokes aesthetics of the Salvadoran landscape, trauma, and (in the case of Hasbun's ixcanal thorns and the Estela Radista embroidery), postmemory.

Themes of gender and sexuality arise in the contemporary art forms that deal directly with the milpa in this chapter. The depiction of plants by women producing items for the sake of representation troubles a binary understanding of gender in the agrarian world. It is not always the cooked food product but the growing plant itself that is embroidered onto a cloth by women depicting wartime violence. The art of Wilber Salguero troubled boundaries between humans and plants, between masculinity and femininity, with Salguero depicting figures that re-member milpas transmitted to the artist by familial memory. These forms of art illustrate a form of vicarious intimacy with the milpa, drawing human attention (both the artist's and viewer's) back to a milpa that was not necessarily cultivated directly by the producer of the art. In Salguero's case, the human being in contact with botanical elements is fluid, in terms of both the humanity and the apparent gender of the subjects. Creative renderings of the milpa among people who are away from it, no longer cultivating it, or who never cultivated it nonetheless return attention to the milpa, above and beyond traditional gender norms surrounding milpa cultivation. These intimacies that are transmitted may reproduce and trouble assumptions of machismo, bringing those assumptions to the forefront of the viewer/reader who considers intimate depictions of milpas from the artists' real, remembered, re-membered, and imagined pasts.

Finally, Caravantes' use of a highly controlled technique (engravings) to represent something random and uncontrollable by the artist (semen, electrocardiograms) connected to people in more-than-human assemblages that produce artefacts with which the artist works asks the viewer/reader to focus on a production process. These methods re-member nonhuman actants in more-than-human assemblages, processing vicarious intimacies between artists and the people in his network. These alterations to and adaptations of established methods may be useful for identifying other contours, dimensions, and depths of more-than-human intimacy in future investigations. Questioning method and experimenting with method can produce innovative renderings of more-than-human intimacies that arise in more-than-human assemblages as they are remembered and re-membered by the artist.

More-than-human intimacies can be felt, perceived, directly observed, examined in interviews, transmitted by stories, and reduced into items that appear on a structured questionnaire. More-than-human intimacies can be evoked, reflected in, and partially transmitted through art. Narratives, words, paint, thread, and statistics may be used to represent more-than-human intimacies, which may be contagious through the medium of the object. The movement of more-than-human intimacies away from more-than-human assemblages calls attention to processes where those intimacies become contagious and jump between human beings in processes of vicarious intimacy. Here, we have tried to think with contemporary Salvadoran artists to understand and imagine vicarious intimacies in action.

SIX

Gastronomic Extractivism

Synopsis

This chapter develops the concept of "gastronomic extractivism," which we define as a process of extracting plant materials from the milpa to feed people at various physical and sociocultural distances from both the milpa and the rural lifeways in which the plant matter is entwined. We explore gradients of gastronomic extractivism based on how the consumed food implicates processes of vicarious intimacies and in-situ conservation. Corn, beans, and squash leave and return to the milpa each year. The seeds, subject to open pollination, are conserved through the dry season. Seeds are then cared for by people who eat what sprouts, and what is harvested is subject to multidimensional extractive processes. Chefs, farmers, and the market economy pull plant matter from the milpa and re-turn it, returning human attention back to the milpa where the plant matter came from. Throughout, we do not argue against nor for alternatives to gastronomic extractivism, but we ask readers to consider gradients of the phenomenon that can be explored through lenses of vicarious intimacy and in-situ conservation.

Corn and Its Pathways of Extraction from the Milpa

To understand gastronomic extractivism, we return our attention to the botanical materials that move away from rural milpas. Corn, beans, and squash are intercropped and are the primary ingredients, among many others, that

FIGURE 6.1 Pupusas being cooked in Olocuilta.

become food products in rural lifeways. Corn plays a central role and is the staple around which much of the logic of human activity on the milpa flows. For now, we will focus on corn. To illustrate gastronomic extractivism and the ways in which it can be evaluated through processes of vicarious intimacy and in-situ conservation, we will myopically follow some trails (Latour 2005) that botanical materials take as they travel away from the milpa.

Corn has been a sacred, central actant, cosmically interpreted as composing human flesh in stories that have been told and retold throughout Central America. In the creation narrative of the Popol Vuh, grandmother Xmucane grinds white corn and yellow corn to generate the flesh of the first humans. Corn is what Xmucane's grandchildren use to give their grandmother a sign of their death and rebirth before they embark on their journey to the underworld Xibalba (Tedlock 1996). The corn dies and is reborn year after year. *Maíz* (corn) is the staple that shapes everyday eating in rural El Salvador, and traditional forms of Salvadoran maíz is longed for from places far away from milpas. One of the initial questions that grounded a line of investigation within this current book was a price conundrum:

Forty pupusas *in* El Salvador = $20
Forty pupusas *in* Colorado *from* El Salvador = $112. (Anastario 2019, 13)

One wonders what it is about those pupusas, so out of place, that makes them worth the 560 percent markup for immigrants to the United States (pupusas are illustrated in figure 6.1). The markup is not truly the cost of the pupusas, since the product is actually a gift and it is the cost of the courier's labor and transport of the parcel that is being paid for (Anastario 2019, 24). Affective processes contribute to the demand for foods made from traditional varieties or for seeds themselves to be sent, and in doing so contribute to the demand for three sisters seeds to be conserved, planted, and regifted. While affective human processes are wound up in the transnational activities of humans who make and deliver these pupusas, there is also something about eating that *maíz de verdad* (real corn), which gives the pupusa a different taste than one made with corn flour purchased in the United States. The smell changes as the corn moves fresh from the husk to its steamed, toasted, liquified, nixtamalized, and cooked outcomes for human consumption. There is something about the taste of that corn that also affects the flesh, becoming embodied through its consumption.

In *Pedagogías de la Muerte* (Pedagogies of Death), the Salvadoran psychoanalyst Jorge Molina provides a surrealist description of a foreign researcher who studies corn and those who surround its growth, where the researcher is cannibalized upon his death by the community with whom he conducted field research. The other-than-human eulogist for the gringo researcher emphasizes that "the most delicious part of the ritual was his blood, luckily days before his blood was completely composed of corn" (Molina 2022, 88). There is something fleshly in stories of corn-human relations in the Central American context. Stories of corn can say something about the ways in which the corn becomes embodied.

We can see corn as an actant that moves and returns to the soil through its more-than-human relations year by year. Each year, a small number of seeds from the best ears are chosen and preserved throughout the dry season for sowing the milpa next year. Molina (2022, 94) writes that "el maíz

FIGURE 6.2 Pupusas being cooked on a comal over fire in Chalatenango.

no selecciona cobardes para renacer" (corn does not select cowards to be reborn), and this passage of corn from one rainy season to the next is a time when much could go wrong. Decades ago, this corn seed would sit in the attic of a tabanco, cured by kitchen smoke coming in from below the attic floorboards (Anastario et al. 2021b), the smoke and the heat serving as a deterrent for weevils, ants, and rodents. Today in Chalatenango, corn seed is often stored in silos or bins, and is sometimes covered in ash, parathion, and/or aluminum phosphide tablets placed below the grain mass to keep weevils, ants, and rodents away. Yet corn is replanted and extracted annually from the ground by those who know how to grow it, including those who eat it. The corn seed moves to places that are physically close and physically far away while demanding that human attention be brought to the conditions of its birth and remaking.

To extract something is to draw something out, to pull or remove it, possibly by force. To extract corn, beans, squash, and other plants from the milpa is to remove plant matter from the milpa, often aided by use of a handheld sickle. Corn stalks are folded and then the ear is torn from the dried stalk, its seeds removed and hauled to homes. Money capable of purchasing food can be a strong force that facilitates the movement of plant matter away from rural spaces. The act of extraction is predicated on corn being subject to human consumption. Many subsistence farmers often find themselves concerned with *eating to live*, and thus *working to eat*. Physical labor is used to take corn from the stalk, to cut bean vines, and to haul squash up and down hills and mountains. Plant matter from the milpa moves on the backs of people who are often seen walking in rubber boots with a machete or sickle in hand on the side of the road, the plant matter stuffed into sacks or bags or onto horses. They may sometimes ask a neighbor in a passing vehicle for a ride, loading the harvest into backs of pickup trucks to get the harvest home. The movement of plant matter to human kitchens is part of the corn's extraction and pathway to rebirth, where humans will select the best seeds and bring them back to the milpa to sow again each rainy season. We think of these forms of movement away from place as physical processes of extraction for gastronomic ends.

While removing botanical materials from the physical space of the milpa is one form of extraction, literally made apparent by the physical distance the plant matter travels away from the milpa, there are also sociocultural dimensions of its extraction. In everyday agrarian lifeways, the corn may move into kitchens and homes only to be brought back to the milpa during the next rainy season, and in twenty-first-century El Salvador the seeds and foodstuffs may periodically be sent as *encomiendas* (parcels) to family members abroad. However, other processes outside of everyday agrarian lifeways are also at play. The extraction of Indigenous plants from Central America was a phenomenon driven by historically colonial and racist forces (Cortez 2018) and informs the ways in which neocolonial forms of extraction occur. Extracting traditional corn and bean varieties from the rural lifeways that have sustained them for the purposes of profit is a form of extraction that not only removes botanical material from place, but engenders out-of-placeness as the object encounters new places where it is demanded by people who may be repelled by the people who grow it and the places where it is grown, at various gradients of removal from the intimacies that were imbricated with its cultivation. We are reminded that power is clever, and that it "produces things, it induces pleasure, forms knowledge, produces discourse" (Foucault 1980, 119). Neocolonial processes of extraction may celebrate and commodify the very rural lifeways from which the plant matter is purchased and extracted, relying on the trope of wholesome campesinos (often living in economic poverty) who have conserved traditional varieties of corn, vending the fruits of their labor to bourgeois audiences who accumulate gastronomic experiences while otherwise having limited and constrained forms of contact with people and plants that have been commodified. There is a growing market and demand for Indigeneity, where "eating the other"—in this case, the Indigenous other—is an experience to be valued and collected by elite consumers (hooks 2015, 21–39). In the Central American context, we find Serena Cosgrove's notion of decolonial intersectionality useful in thinking about the sociocultural location of the eater relative to the lifeways from which the traditional variety emerged. Cosgrove (2020) combines intersectionality (articulating how unequal structures disempower and marginalize while igniting agency, leadership, and resistance) with decoloniality (acknowledging the colonial past, decolonization of independence, and ongoing resistance) to account for oppression while recognizing persistence in a Central American context, encouraging both a reflexive and critical analysis that moves beyond modeling identity-based deficits. Decolonial intersectionality allows us to simultaneously think consciously about the position of the eater and the survival of the traditional cultivar without escaping or removing ourselves from processes of extraction. When thinking about the distances between the milpa and the eater, we also consider the vicarious intimacies that are shared and how the act of consumption may or may not contribute to the in-situ conservation of a traditional cultivar. A good question for the analyst to ask is the likelihood of whether the eater of the corn product would offer a vehicular ride to the milpa farmer who is trying to haul the harvest away from the milpa. Considering these questions helps bring sociocultural dimensions of extraction into relief.

Gastronomic extractivism is thus a multidimensional concept that we use to understand gradients of a necessarily extractive human process, characterized by its relationship with processes of vicarious intimacy and its ability to reinforce in-situ conservation. We examine these relations by exploring three "gradients" of gastronomic extractivism represented in this chapter as "cases." We do not think of these gradients of gastronomic extractivism as reflecting a linear process, nor do we propose an escape from or alternative to the process. We attempt to stay with the trouble (Haraway 2016), in this case troubled processes of eating. We sort the cases by physical distance traveled from the milpa. We begin by exploring gastronomic extractivism in the context of the Salvadoran diaspora, which represents the furthest physical distance that plant matter travels from the milpa relative to the other cases we present. Then, we shift focus to the much more physically proximate, but socially troublesome, culinary scene in the urban capital San Salvador. Finally, we examine processes of extraction in the context of rural lifeways where ingredients are more traceable to the intimacies entangled with their cultivation, and the actual places where the descendants of traditional cultivars will be recultivated.

Diasporic Longing and In-situ Conservation

Seeds from traditional cultivars are sometimes sent as encomiendas, or parcels, to Salvadoran migrants in diasporic strongholds throughout the United States (Anastario 2019, 6). Seeking out traditional cultivars is not unique to Salvadoran migrants; migrants and seeds often go together (Nazarea 2005, 65). Corn seeds sent as encomiendas from El Salvador are often turned into food products once inside the United States (as opposed to being planted in the United States, which sometimes occurs in processes of trans-situ conservation, but which is not the focus of this case analysis). The gastronomic demand within the Salvadoran diaspora often fosters and reinforces intimacy between people involved in the seed's cultivation and contributes to the in-situ cultivation of the seeds in El Salvador.

Salvadoran corn seed is longed for from abroad in milpa farmers' diasporic networks. Maíz blanco and maíz negro are sometimes sent with couriers from the Salvadoran countryside to make atole and tortillas. It is often surprising to see such a large amount of money paid to ship such a small amount of traditional corn seeds that are often exchanged in Chalatenango as gifts, free of charge. Mateo, a courier who travels between Chalatenango and the United States, described how people will send/receive five pounds of corn seed to make ten to twenty tortillas to alleviate their nostalgia in Colorado where his clients are based:

Hay unos molinos pequeños. . . . La gente procesa ese maíz en el molino y se produce la masa. Ese sentimiento de nostalgia les florece. Entonces no quieren Maseca. . . . Yo pienso que al final ese pedido que la gente hace no es para cocinar en masa, es para aliviar el sentimiento de nostalgia que tiene.

There are some small [corn] grinders . . . People process that corn in the grinder and that's how they make the dough. That feeling of nostalgia blooms in them. So, they don't want "Maseca" [a brand name of corn flour]. . . . In the end, people are not trying to cook a large quantity of anything, it's to alleviate the feeling of nostalgia that they have.

Making ten to twenty tortillas is not a significant quantity in El Salvador, but it is a significant activity to request these ingredients from abroad and to render Salvadoran food from Salvadoran-grown ingredients within the confines of the United States. Mateo emphasizes that "lo que tiene el valor de ese traslado de maíz es que es maíz de verdad" (the value in bringing the corn all that way is that it's real corn). *Real corn* from El Salvador is what is demanded, not the corn available in North American grocery stores. That real Salvadoran corn is moved by diasporic demand, and its materialization alleviates human nostalgia for fleeting moments in the diaspora. That diasporic longing may reflect a type of intimacy that does not seek to return home (restorative nostaliga), but that longs for the making of a new home in the diasporic present (reflective nostalgia) (Boym 2008). It is also a longing that is often intimately connected, within diasporic networks, to farmers and farming families cultivating the traditional seed itself, in home gardens or alongside the margins of milpas. The longing connects migrants abroad to farmers at home through processes of vicarious intimacy that are reinforced by family and friends sending food parcels derived from Salvadoran milpas that alleviate nostalgias in the diaspora. Sometimes the U.S.-based family members send remittances, and sometimes those remittances are used to make improvements to the milpa where traditional cultivars are cultivated (Arias Rodas 2019).

The demand for ingredients from the milpa is not just to make tortillas. Many of Mateo's rural migrant clientele in the United States long for flavors derived from plants cultivated in El Salvador (Anastario 2019, 58). Rural Salvadorans send *harina de maíz blanco* (white corn flour) to make hot *atol de maíz blanco* (white corn atole). Sometimes, his clients in Chalatenango place *atol de elote* (a creamy type of corn atole) in a plastic bag and Mateo freezes it like *charramusca* (little plastic bags of flavored milk that get tied up, frozen, and then eaten from the corner). These forms of atole in the United States must be defrosted and consumed as individual servings, as opposed to being prepared and ladled out from large metal canisters. Mateo also has a client in Boulder, Colorado, who regularly asks for ten to fifteen pounds of *frijoles desgranado* (shelled beans) from Chalatenango to steam or use in pupusas. The desire that moves small quantities of traditional cultivars abroad is one that is entangled with rural nostalgia, economic demand, and familial affiliations with cultivators of traditional corn in El Salvador (Anastario 2019, 16–33). Especially when requested by migrants who have worked the milpa, the intimacy shared between family members across borders is a type of vicarious intimacy that stokes attention and affect for the Salvadoran milpa back home. Even after migrating, some Salvadorans still manage home gardens, replete with small plots of corn grown using the lunar cycle, in suburban backyards of the United States. But this garden *aquí* (in the United States) is never quite like the milpa *allá* (in Chalatenango). The desire for traditional corn sent from family in Chalatenango provokes family members and friends in El Salvador to continue cultivating those seed varieties that will be sent with a courier to the United States. Vicarious intimacy plays a role in facilitating connections and requests. Familiar plant matter is extracted from the milpa by relatives before it travels a very far distance away, across national boundaries, in routine cycles of extraction that result in the production of food products consumed abroad. The desire abroad is contingent with intimacies between relatives separated by diasporic divides that returns attention to the milpa. This gradient of gastronomic extractivism is one that relies on and stokes vicarious intimacy among people split by diasporic divides and fosters the in-situ conservation of traditional varieties on Salvadoran milpas at home. These elements of intimacy and conservation recur, despite the massive physical divides between Salvadorans *aquí* and *allá*.

Haute Traditional Food in the Urban Capital

This description and ethnographic experience of "high cuisine" involving traditional cultivars is defined by multiple failed efforts of the authors to access haute traditional food in El Salvador. This ethnographic experience of failure marks the nascent emergence of haute traditional cuisine in San Salvador and the conditions that make it so exclusive. This case is focused on an eating experience where the physical distance between the milpa and the eater is much shorter than the distance traveled by botanical materials in diasporic networks, but where the sociocultural distances between the eater and the milpa farmers are appreciable. This case is focused on the emergence of haute traditional cuisine in San Salvador, where there are notable breaches in vicarious intimacy among eaters, and where in-situ conservation is driven by processes of cultural commodification. The eater, in the Central American context, must be able to afford the price markup that is paid not to a family member or individual in a close-knit network but, rather, to a chef and restaurant that brokers access to traditional cultivars through the commodification of the food's traditionality/Indigeneity.

While urban centers in El Salvador have ample cafeterias, restaurants that serve *comida a la vista* (cafeteria-style service), pupuserías, and food vending stations at *mercados* (markets), this analysis is not focused on them. It is focused on the emergence of haute cuisine in San Salvador that caters to an elite clientele, and more specifically on "haute traditional" food that is recontextualized as elite cuisine and served in venues such as expensive restaurants, simultaneously marginalizing those who cultivate the ingredients and who traditionally make the dishes (Sammells 2019). The exclusivity of the venue is reinforced by Elena and Mike being unable to obtain a seat at a table during their 2022 stay in San Benito, an upscale enclave of San Salvador where the country's wealthy and elite maintain apartments, houses, and businesses. The concept of gastronomic extractivism first came into relief as Elena and Mike first complained to one another, and then began to make conjectures about why they were unable to get a seat.

Following their inability to get a reservation, Elizabeth re-turned this chapter and returned to San Benito with the goal of obtaining a reservation in 2023. Her first inquiry was met with a response that the restaurant was only serving private functions while in the process of changing locations, and she was offered a six-course meal at $65 per head, for a minimum of six people ($390 total). Sixty-five dollars is economically equivalent to roughly eight days of hired milpa labor in Chalatenango and more than five days of the professional minimum wage in San Salvador in 2023. The cost of the entire meal for the required minimum number of diners would have been equivalent to nearly ten weeks of farm labor in the Chalateco countryside. Given the prime location of the restaurant and the labor of the chefs and waitstaff, the costs are presumed to cover overhead costs and wages, and we are unaware of how economically profitable the endeavor is. While Elizabeth, in the name of research, was willing to pay that price for herself and her husband, she couldn't think of four other people who might be willing and able to comprise the rest of the dinner party.

A few months later, Elizabeth tried again, and after a failed attempt (being told the restaurant was fully booked), she managed to get a reservation for two on a Saturday night; having a toddler at home, she requested the earliest possible reservation, at 6:00 p.m. She pulled into the parking lot right behind a car with diplomatic plates, and for the first part of the evening, the only other diners were obviously foreigners, many of them casually dressed. As the night wore on, some Salvadoran diners arrived; they were noticeably more dressed up. The entrance to the restaurant was not well marked, and nearly all the diners (including Elizabeth) missed it upon first arriving, leading the host, dressed in a blue blazer, to repeatedly run outside to flag people down and beckon them back to the door.

The menu included a mix of traditional dishes and international dishes sourced from Salvadoran ingredients (such as "naan de maíz"), with a nod to high and low culture (the drinks menu included a $105 bottle of champagne as well as a $6 "Regia Chola," a large bottle of local beer). One wall was decorated with a screen made of *tusas* (corn husks), while another showcased a traditional grinding stone to prepare corn, a basket for cooked tortillas, and a pot for tamales. Tortillas made of *maíz criollo* (creole corn) were served in a basket wrapped in traditional fabric, and their blue color was lined by a row of sliced *pipián* (a type of squash) that grows amid cornrows in milpas (figure 6.5). The blue hue of the tortillas was pointed out by the server as a sign of their specialness and authenticity.

One *tamal de chipilín*, a traditional tamale dish made of *masa de maíz* (corn dough) and a leafy local legume, cost ten dollars; Elizabeth's husband at first resisted ordering it, because "my aunt makes that." While beautifully garnished and flavorful, it felt strange to divide a single tamal between two people in an air-conditioned space, instead of gathered around a large table with multiple generations of family members talking over one another, fanning themselves, swatting away flies, and throwing discarded husks to be licked clean by animals. In the countryside, tamales often appear in stacks stuffed into a *huacal* (large container) and appear in piles on plates at rural kitchen tables. The single tamal underscored the haute cuisine approach to an everyday tamal.

The difficulty the authors experienced in getting a reservation and the high cost of dining reflect the commodification of traditional cultivars for an elite, urban consumer. The ingredients were marketed as uniquely local, Salvadoran, and of this place to a consuming public that, devoid of intimate relationships with farmworkers or milpas producing these ingredients, demands haute traditional food. While some type of vicarious intimacy likely exists between the cultivators and the chefs (who were not interviewed), the consumer's experience of eating is devoid of a range of vicarious intimacies that could be shared with those who cultivated the ingredients from a milpa. What is left is the experience of presentation of the food and its flavor, which is important to farmers but leaves consumers with an opaque experience of milpa farming, milpa farmers, and the more-than-human intimacies therein. The economic demand for the product likely contributes, through ongoing purchase of the ingredients, to the in-situ conservation of these cultivars. The fact that the restaurant is not more accessible and in greater demand also signifies experimentation with a new concept and limited local demand for it. This analysis is in no way intended to criticize or undermine the work of the chefs, and we recognize their innovation and creativity in experimenting with and creating delicious haute traditional Salvadoran cuisine. As we think with Cosgrove's (2020) lens of decolonial intersectionality, we wonder if the clientele they market their food to would be willing to stop a vehicle in the countryside and pick up farmers walking alongside the road, replete with their machetes and harvest, to haul traditional cultivars from their milpas to rural homes and markets. Traditionality and the milpa are simulated, at high cost and in the safety of a fine dining environment, for economically elite diners. The physical distance the botanical material traveled from the milpa to the urban capital is shorter than the international trip that food makes in the diaspora (described in the case above). However, the sociocultural distances between the culinary scene (the location of the restaurant and the clientele it serves) and the rural lifeways from which traditional cultivars emerged are vast and marked by a relatively limited potential for vicarious intimacy to emerge amid eaters of traditional haute cuisine.

Traditional Food in Rural Lifeways

In agrarian lifeways, botanical material is repeatedly extracted from the milpa and is moved into home kitchens by the people responsible for its cultivation. Farm-to-kitchen travel patterns for plant matter from the milpa may be facilitated by farmers or those who do work peripheral to the milpa, like a mother responsible for making tortillas who visits the family milpa to peel back the husk of maíz blanco and inhale the sweet, green smell of the corn, collecting some of it in a basket and hauling it back with her daughters and in-laws. Rural home kitchens were places that the ethnographer regularly traversed during fieldwork, often forgetting to remove his rubber boots and then apologizing to the women who managed kitchens for trudging soil from the milpa onto the floor as he followed other farmers who did the same. Rural home kitchens were places where botanical matter from the milpa is transformed by people directly connected to those who cultivated it. Rural home kitchens and outdoor woodfire *comals* (griddles) were sites where processes of vicarious intimacy took place (figure 6.2).

As corn, beans, and squash from the milpa were being cooked by a family member or friend, their recent past might be talked about, often with the person who cultivated the ingredient. This too affects the culinary experience of the food in rural lifeways. The ethnographer experienced a critical moment when he was served pupusas that were made from maiz blanco, frijoles de seda, and ayote. There was no fanfare or special occasion, and the ethnographer was still wearing a sweaty work shirt as he ate them with his bare hands. Laura (the cook) commented that the ethnographer had observed the cultivation of all the ingredients from the pupusa he was eating. Laura knew exactly where the ingredients came from and who cultivated them. She was also recounting a tale of having observed the observer. Sitting with the ethnographer was Chepe, who planted the ingredients in his milpita. The pupusas were cooked with firewood that would generate ash for the second fertilization of his milpita. The pungent odor of the *quesillo* (a type of cheese) was balanced by the smooth flavors of the maiz blanco and ayote, which tasted smokey from being cooked on an outdoor, woodfire comal. The circularity of the farm-to-table production cycle in this case required no exchange of money for the corn, beans, and squash ingredients, but the flavors underscored the varieties that Chepe held onto and cultivated in his own milpita. Back stories were known that were connected to the experience of eating and taste. As they ate, and in response to Laura's comment, the ethnographer felt awkwardly compelled to talk about the ingredients as though he was a eulogist for the plant parts being eaten. He remembered aloud the *ayotillo* (little squash) that grew into the big ayote, the one they were eating. Chepe, the cultivator of the ingredients in the pupusa who taught the ethnographer that curious word (ayotillo), laughed at him for being such a ridiculous gringo, and then Laura could not help herself and began laughing. The flavor memory of that three sisters pupusa was rich with ridiculous laughter among those implicated in every aspect of its production. Laura then mentioned that we would soon be eating the ingredients from the milpa that Mike was still cultivating on his milpa.

The above scenario is an affective example of what David Sutton (2001, 28) describes of food as being integral to the genesis of prospective memories, orienting the eaters to future memories surrounding the consumption of food. The temporality, affinities, and memory of nonhumans in this practice of food is everyday. It is shared between humans who are wound up in agrarian lifeways, requiring human-plant relationships to produce the vicarious intimacy that was shared among the humans who cultivate/eat plants grown in the milpa.

The type of vicarious intimacy that was experienced in the everyday while eating in rural lifeways was also marked by moments of synesthesia, which refers to coupled or joined sensations (Cytowic 2018). Waking up to go to the milpa at 4:00 a.m., the ethnographer chugged coffee before work, and then ate breakfast about four hours later. One day, after the team finished *chapodando* (trimming) with a cuma at 8:00 a.m., they sat down under the large guayaba tree in the center of the milpa to eat the breakfast the brothers' mother brought down to the field for them (figure 6.3). The ingredients had traveled away from the milpa to be converted into food and returned to the milpa for human consumption. The ingredients were made from seeds the brothers had cultivated the year prior, the same seeds that were related to the corn stalks growing around them as they ate their ancestors. They were given a generous serving of frijoles de seda, requesón, three tortillas made from maíz blanco, and a chili pepper that the brothers referred to as "chilpepe" (also known as *chiltepe*) to eat with their hands. Mike bit into the pepper and was overwhelmed by the heat, along with the flood of visuals rooted in memories that had become his experience of chiltepe. He remembered plastic packets filled with orange and ruby fluid and objects, sent as a parcel from Chalatenango to Aurora, Colorado. He remembered a pupuseria that served something with pupusas that he could not quite remember. The taste of chiltepe was longing, memory, laughter, the smell of petrol alongside the pupuseria, and the essence of *escabeche*, a type of pickled cabbage that is often served with pupusas. But this flavor, produced with something a farmer had collected during milpa farming, was capable of producing those affective/reflective processes as they quickly ate their breakfasts with their hands while seated in the grass on a milpa in Chalatenango. The ethnographer said

FIGURE 6.3 Farmers after eating breakfast on a milpa, women carrying food supplies away.

that the chiltepe tasted like escabeche, and one of the farmers vigorously nodded his head. This experience illustrates what Sutton (2001, 102) refers to as the synesthetic qualities of food as ingredients "in ritual and everyday experiences of totality," where the memories of taste and smell may be idiosyncratic but are nonetheless illuminated by the associative fields in which they are experienced and learned. The youngest of the brothers repeatedly offered chiltepe during morning breakfasts, chiltepe that he had collected as he encountered it growing wild. It was a type of shared recognition between people regarding a landrace variety of chili pepper and that the young farmer took the time to collect to compliment his breakfasts of tortilla, beans, and cheese every day.

Vicarious intimacies occur between those who cultivate milpas and those closely connected individuals who transform plant matter into food. As plant matter was followed into rural kitchens, including kitchens used to generate pupusas for sale, the local spirituality of rural milpa farmers also came into view. In some kitchens, there were pictures and/or stories told of Óscar Romero visiting the town in 1979 (figure 6.4). Romero is a polarizing figure in contemporary El Salvador. As described in chapter 1, Romero was a Catholic bishop who advocated for the rural poor and who was assassinated in 1980. He was later canonized (as a Catholic saint) in 2018. Romero's own pastoral language was rich with seed metaphors: his famous line, "Let my blood be a seed of freedom," is often repeated as his martyrdom is commemorated (Romero et al. 1980). He was frequently mentioned by farmers, including Gerardo who, in chapter 3, presented researchers with *chilipuca* seeds from lineages that had been blessed by Romero before his assassination. Everyday foods like atole, riguas, and pupusas were haunted by images and memories of Óscar Romero before he was assassinated. Gerardo described how he then

> bendijo los granos y él . . . ese día que él vino esa calle ahí la llenaron toda, fuimos a cortar maíz y cada mata íbamos sembrando como el suelo con una barra íbamos sembrando matas por toda la calle como acá y entonces ahí venía él por toda esa calle la gente venía detrás de él. Hicieron atol, rigua, tortita de elote todo y se dio eso gratis, hasta el día de hoy esa fiesta la hacemos en agosto gratis. Hemos invitado a gente de Cuba, viene gente de mucho país, nosotros le hacemos la invitación que vengan porque ahí usted viene a tomar atol gratis y come elotes cocido gratis, asado, rigua, gratis ahí no se vende porque lo hacemos en una conmemoración a él que vino ese día, bendijo los granos y gracias a Dios donde nosotros ha habido secas de un mes, de 18 días, y las milpas gracias a Dios siempre han producido, aunque sea poco, siempre han producido, nunca hemos tenido una perdida.

FIGURE 6.4 Photograph of Óscar Romero's local visit hanging on a wall in a pupuseria in Chalatenango.

blessed the grains and he . . . that day he came up that street over there and they filled it all up [with corn], we went to cut corn and we planted corn up and down the street like right here, and he came up the street from over there and people walked behind him. They made atole, rigua, tortita de elote and they gave it out for free, and since then we've had that same celebration where everything is given out for free. We have invited people from Cuba, people come from many countries, we invite them to come because that's when you come to drink atole for free and eat cooked corn for free, roasted corn, rigua, it is all free and it is not sold because we do it in commemoration of the day he came to us, blessed the seeds and thank God, we've had droughts that were a month long, 18 days long, and thank God the milpas have always produced even if it is only a little, they have always produced, we have never had a loss.

The roasted corn, riguas, and atole, which Gerardo emphasized were free of charge, are often based on ingredients that may be made from seeds derived from those blessed by Romero in 1979. Even if they were not, the memory of seeds blessed by Romero is wound up, through Gerardo's continued open pollination of traditional corn and bean varieties, in the food items given away for free four decades later. Gerardo's story is also an intimate retelling of how in-situ conservation and human memories connect directly to eating traditional foods in Chalatenango. The traditional varieties of corn and beans blessed by Romero are consumed as food and replanted each year, the significance of the collective memory contributing to their in-situ conservation. The farmer still cultivates and gifts the descendants of these seeds to friends in the community and outside visitors like our research team, retelling the story and stoking vicarious intimacies as Gerardo continues to experience more-than-human intimacies in the milpa he cultivates with lineages of seeds blessed by Romero.

The gastronomic extractivism defined in the eating of everyday traditional food in agrarian lifeways is one where physical movement of botanical materials from the milpa to the kitchen is facilitated by the same people who share experiences of more-than-human intimacies with the milpa. It is the case with which the ethnographer was most familiar, and which served as a point of contradistinction for thinking through gastronomic extractivism in the other cases. These cases are not static, and there may be points of overlap and connection between them. We have separated them out to more clearly articulate what gastronomic extractivism is, and to illustrate how it may implicate processes of vicarious intimacy and in-situ conservation.

Transcending Cases with the Mirada Fuerte

Our analysis of gastronomic extractivism offers no alternative or escape. The farm-to-table and slow food movements of the elite do not offer alternatives to the phenomena of botanical material being physically extracted from the milpa for the purposes of human consumption, traveling various physical and sociocultural distances away from the more-than-human assemblage of milpa farming. Rather, gastronomic extractivism offers a lens that can be used to think about traditional varieties that are consumed, and is a concept that can be expanded upon, modified, or potentially applied elsewhere. We do not expect the three cases we identified to serve as fixed categories or referents for future studies; rather, they are illustrative of varying "gradients" of gastronomic extractivism. These gradients do not occur in completely separate social and cultural spheres. As a way of illustrating transcendence between cases, we re-turn a final anecdote that persisted across cases but which we bracketed out for the purposes of illustration. It concerns the transmission of recipes that facilitate processes of vicarious intimacy between those who sensuously attune to ingredients derived from the milpa.

In collecting recipes that involved corn-based ingredients from people close to milpas, the most common caveat provided by the transmitter of the recipe was that nobody with a mirada fuerte—"a strong gaze"—should prepare the food. This warning was given during air-conditioned car rides by highly educated people in San Salvador, in rural kitchens, and in U.S.-based kitchens where Salvadoran migrants made traditional foods from ingredients sent from Chalatenango with a courier. In folk medicine, it is assumed that someone with a mirada fuerte can, unintentionally, cause an infant to become sick with diarrhea, vomit, and experience high bodily temperatures by simply looking at the infant (Erquicia Cruz and Herrera Reina 2014). Someone who was the victim of maldiojo (mal de ojo, or "bad eyes," the recipient of the mirada fuerte) can then retain the effect of the gaze and also transmit their infliction to other humans over their lifespan. When it comes to food preparation, someone with a mirada fuerte should not be allowed to stir atole made from corn (because it will ruin the atole), nor can they beat eggs (because the eggs will become watery) or engage in other cooking activities, particularly when whisking and stirring activities are involved.

After collecting one recipe for torreja served with *chilate* (a type of yolk bread soaked in sugarcane syrup served with a corn atole used to dull the sweetness), Laura warned that someone with a mirada fuerte should not be allowed to beat the eggs. The recipe is translated into English, but we retain some of Laura's original expressions in Spanish to provide greater detail and context for how the recipe was transmitted.

Recipe from Laura to Make Torrejas with Chilate

TORREJAS

Ingredients

    Pan de yema (yolk bread)

    2 atado de dulce (hardened blocks of crushed sugar cane juice)

    4 eggs

    Pepper

Oil

Limón

Cinnamon

White vanilla

Directions

To start, you have to have the right bread. You either have to use yolk bread or yolk cake. Beat 4 eggs. Mix in limón, ground cinnamon, and white vanilla. You have to beat the eggs until they are white like snow. If someone has a mirada fuerte, that person cannot beat the eggs. The eggs will become watery if someone with a mirada fuerte beats the eggs. Soak the bread in the mixture. This process is called *calzar el pan*. Pour a little bottle of oil into the soaking bread mixture. Then you have to prepare the atado de dulce. In 4 cups of boiling water, you put two atado de dulce and mix them together. Put the bread and honey together into a larger pan (Pyrex). Afterward, you can eat it immediately, but you have to drink it with chilate, because the torreja is sweet, and the chilate is the refreshment that is meant to accompany it.

CHILATE

Ingredients

2 spoonfuls of *maíz de harina blanco* (white corn flour)

1 liter of water

Pimiento gorda (pepper)

Ginger

Directions

Mix 2 spoonfuls of maíz de harina blanco into one liter of water. Boil it so that *no hace daño* ("it doesn't do harm [to the stomach]"). Put pimiento gorda and a piece of mashed ginger into the mix.

When looking for other recipes, ones that were subject to more forgetting such as *chachama* (a sweet type of corn bread) and *quesadilla de maíz* (traditional Salvadoran corn bread similar to pound cake), the recipes were transmitted to the authors with reminders that women who are menstruating should not be allowed to beat the eggs, nor should anyone with a mirada fuerte.

What is notable about the recipes provided is that they involve corn and a warning not to let anyone with a mirada fuerte participate in certain food

FIGURE 6.5 Pipián (squash), overgrown to extract seeds and save them for the next rainy season.

preparation activities. Elena Salamanca personally laments her inability to beat eggs due to having received a maldiojo during her childhood. When she was a child, the women in Elena's family kept her out of the kitchen during the preparation of meals, leading to what she considers to be a breach in the transmission of culinary memory for those affected by maldiojo in the past.

She was unable to directly learn many traditional recipes because she was not permitted to observe them being made by her family members due to their fear of Elena ruining the recipe with her mirada fuerte. Elena emphasizes that families with just one girl who was subject to maldiojo are at the greatest risk for such recipes to not be transmitted and thus ultimately lost within family lines.

While these intimate warnings about the preparation of food abounded as we sought out traditional recipes and foods, it is also worth noting that some milpa farmers place amulets or tie red ribbons onto trees near their milpas to stave off the effect that someone with a mirada fuerte might have on the growing milpa while passing by. Much like the preparation of food derived from the milpa, some consider that the growing plants within the milpa are just as vulnerable to the unintended effects of someone with a strong gaze looking upon them. It is not that the person with a mirada fuerte intentionally ruins the milpa, it is just something that is perceived as being transmittable from humans to plants, humans to food, and from humans to other humans. These everyday intimacies concerning food and plants are shared between people who cultivate, prepare, and eat them, cognizant of multispecies vulnerabilities and the effects of humans who gaze upon nonhumans. In this way, the mirada fuerte serves as a metaphor and for thinking through potential distances between gazers, plants, farmers, and the people who prepare and consume the food, and it also serves as a metaphor for thinking about the transmissibility of vicarious intimacy in more-than-human assemblages.

Conclusion

Gastronomic extractivism concerns the movement of botanical materials away from the milpa for the purposes of human consumption. Thinking through the physical distances that traditional seeds travel from their ancestors, particularly for the purposes of being eaten, is one way to approach the material dimension of gastronomic extractivism. As botanical material physically moves away from the milpa, physical distance from the milpa and sociocultural distances of the cooked product from the agrarian lifeway should be considered. The experience or possibility of vicarious intimacy and the contribution of eating patterns to in-situ conservation will characterize gradients of gastronomic extractivism.

Considering the sociocultural distance from which the consumer stands relative to the milpa, in the Central American context, can be aided by Cosgrove's notion of decolonial intersectionality (Cosgrove 2020). One must be cognizant of unequal structures that disempower while simultaneously thinking through the colonial past associated with the extraction of traditional cultivars, and whether the gastronomic effort is contributing to the survival of both the cultivar and the lifeway in which it is being cultivated by milpa farmers. While we offer no escape from gastronomic extractivism, we do wonder if there are ways that those with more social and economic levels of privilege could be leveraging some of their privilege in the name of survivance, in this case facilitating efforts to support the in-situ conservation of traditional varieties and recognition of the people responsible for conserving and cultivating them. We remind readers that in its applied context, gastronomic extractivism is not something to escape or to avoid, but to conscientiously navigate.

We have tried to elucidate how gastronomic extractivism is a concept that can be used to understand the removal of botanical materials from the milpa and can be characterized by contingent relations of the eater with vicarious intimacy and in-situ conservation. We consider it to be a useful concept for thinking about and being conscious of the plants that one is eating, the affective processes behind the cultivators of the plants and the cooks responsible for rendering them into food, and the survival of plants and people assembled in Salvadoran milpa farming.

Conclusion

"As I start a new chapter, it's like I've never written before."

—IRINA CARLOTA SILBER, ANTHROPOLOGIST
(PERS. COMM., NOVEMBER 21, 2019)

Patterns of vicarious intimacies have emerged as more-than-human intimacies in milpa farming, and vicarious intimacies have patterned reiterations of the more-than-human assemblage that is milpa farming. Patterns of vicarious intimacies have washed over and into us as researchers, thinkers, and writers. Our vicarious intimacies have in turn patterned the ways in which we attuned to, sampled, examined, analyzed, wrote about, and represented the cultivation of the three sisters in Chalatenango and El Salvador. Cultivating the three sisters affects those who cultivate the three sisters, which affects those who cultivate the three sisters . . .

This exploration of more-than-human intimacies on the Salvadoran milpa focused on how nonhuman plants assemble with humans who reproduce plants over time as plant matter moves through human spaces. This work was an inductive endeavor predicated on the use of a method concerned with the act of recuperating. Recuperative observation was a starting point for a research activity that led to resampling and re-turning concepts concerning affective processes that circulate as one is actively doing something while gazing backward in time. Cultivating traditional varieties of the three sisters on milpas is an intimate endeavor that brings one's gaze into multiple pasts. At times, this study focused on intimacies between people as they cultivated and consumed plants from the milpa, while at other times it explicitly focused on methods used to study intimacies surrounding human-plant relations.

Throughout this work, we have tried to remember Bruno Latour's (2005, 174) "clamps" that keep the social world flat, asking "any candidate with a more 'global' role to sit beside the 'local' site it claims to explain, rather than watch it jump on top of it or behind it." After retelling a history of the Salvadoran milpa (chapter 1), we explored methodological alterations to ethnographic practice (chapter 2) and we subsequently explained some of the findings that flowed from those altered methodological approaches (chapter 3). This led to us refocusing on methods that elicit life histories (chapter 4), as well as giving us focal points for thinking about the ways in which plant matter travels through networks of humans who represent (chapter 5) and eat (chapter 6) the plant matter relative to processes of vicarious intimacy and the in-situ conservation of traditional cultivars in El Salvador. This is an analysis inspired by the act of re-turning subject matter, not developing a linear line of investigation defined by predetermined research questions, nor illustrating the global significance of local findings. It offers no radical alternatives and no routes of escape. It is a looping way of thinking and researching, of re-turning human-plant relations practiced by rural farmworkers and imagined by those in close and distal relations with them. The findings reported in this book are like nodes on a rhizome, each growing and developing in nonlinear ways and in relation to more-than-human intimacies of the Salvadoran milpa. Intra-acting with and developing that space, we have tried to provide symmetric attention to method and concept throughout.

Solidarity in Methodology

People tell stories about their lives and the recent past, and sometimes people tell stories to researchers as a way of teaching the researchers something that people perceive to be worth looking into. This type of storytelling is not necessarily an act that we have interpreted as one governed by the purest intention of *helping the researcher*, but rather one that *alters the researcher's gaze*. The altered gaze may reveal a new area of inquiry that storytellers perceive to be important, even if that importance is not elaborated in the form of an academic hypothesis, or especially when everyday hypotheses embedded in storytelling begin to haunt the researcher.

This is a study grounded in method and attention to method. The methods are useful in that they attune the researcher to more-than-human assemblages and their emergent properties in an agrarian lifeway. We have tried to illustrate ways in which research directions can shift as people make suggestions to an ethnographer and as objects move through the spaces they examine. The style of milpa farming that is practiced today in Chalatenango has changed rapidly over the course of the past one hundred years. The contingencies between soils, forests, microclimates, traditional cultivars, the use of fire and smoke, agrichemicals, and farmers' health have altered and shifted with time. Some of these changes are remembered by older farmers who still understand the systems of land rotation and rest that were conducted through fire and fallow methods, which are widely stigmatized today. Those who remember these systems continue to engage in the in-situ conservation of traditional cultivars in El Salvador, with little to no economic support for doing so. The method underlying the ethnographic data produced in this book, recuperative observation, was intended to leverage and stoke these memories while involving farmers in the act of research. Farmers raised interesting questions and pointed some of them directly at the research team. We sat with that discomfort and, to the best of our ability, tried to grow with it. Long stories about agrichemicals past and present inform farmers' questions of whether the chemicals are killing people. As "participant observers" with access to phones, education, research instruments, and the internet, we researchers sometimes must ask ourselves how we can contribute, methodologically, in solidarity. Decolonizing methods is an active process, where one must be doing something (collecting data) in ways that will undoubtedly produce dreaded mistakes, biting peer reviews, and shame. Decolonizing methods occurs in messy and everyday ways for researchers as they are in the field, and may sometimes entail researchers losing their grip on original research aims and, more broadly, their "purpose." Being open to changing research directions, adjusting and adapting methods that are responsive to stories being told by participants, relinquishing some investigational authorities, and allowing people to accomplish their own aims (that may *never* be published!) in a small space temporarily generated by the researcher's privilege are methodological practices we can cultivate, test, and evaluate amid calls for decolonizing methods. We used the term "recuperative observation" to refer to an adapted style of participant observation that was practiced emphasizing coinvolvement that may be useful in multiple ways that extend beyond notions of sustainability or formulas of representation in participatory research strategies. Research methods can feel conceptually invariant in the mind of the researcher at times, and changing methods during a study may feel scandalous or too unruly. Much like the attention to method inherent to the art of Efraín Caravantes (chapter 5), there are times when the researcher must confront and consider intimate subject matter, contemplating multiple origin stories and processes of representation. Recuperative observation asks that the participant observer alter the method according to information provided by the observed. Knowing through interaction with storytellers can sometimes require that we change the ways in which we practice documenting the stories that are told, particularly when we feel that the stories are being told to us because we carry privilege with access to information about ailments like chronic kidney disease of unknown origin and acute pesticide poisoning. Altering a method to see something that is being recounted, even if it is inconvenient for the researcher, is one way to work in methodological solidarity that may be responsive to a request that comes in the form of a direct question or everyday hypothesis among interlocuters.

The Writing Process / Acts of Representation

An altered method responsive to storytelling still results in the production of data that contribute to the generation of knowledge and understanding. Contemporary concerns about representation, cognitive extractivism, and decoloniality at times paralyzed the process of writing the ethnographic data that appear in this book. Marilyn Strathern writes about how the preoccupations of anthropologists take a bifurcated turn:

> They argue about how to interpret the meaning of the actions, artefacts, words and so on produced by the people they study, understood as values and qualities that people thereby represent to themselves. Simultaneously they argue about how the ethnographer represents these meanings in the art of writing. (2004a, 7)

Moving beyond a writing paralysis caused by concerns regarding representation surrounding more-than-human intimacies was a challenge. To move beyond it, we looked to see what others were doing and how they were thinking. The ethnographic work of anthropologist Irina Carlota Silber has troubled what for many are romantic, totalizing, and homogenizing images of freedom-fighting campesinos. In the later arc of her research in Chalatenango, Silber (2022) wrote about an ethics of collective care premised on an affective response to *debilidad* (weakness) experienced by others. The impulse to automatically assist the sick and wounded, including animals showing signs of debilidad, offered radical ways for thinking about who cares about who, or who cares about what. The ethics that Silber (2022) explicated encouraged acknowledgement of the ethnographer's intimacy of *compromiso* (commitment) to the subject matter at hand. Intimate commitment to subject matter that concerns nonhumans, in our case, contributed to the conceptualization of vicarious intimacies that move between networks of people (including researchers) who are in contact with the more-than-human intimacies of the Salvadoran milpa. Intimate commitment to subject matter also means that our study would detour into methods for measuring human-chemical interactions when farmers die young and other farmers ask researchers questions about causes of illness and death in remote, rural places. Paying critical attention to the intimacies of the ethnographer in the act of writing about an ethics of collective care in Chalatenango helped us move beyond the paralysis of reflexivity. We reconsider the intimate and everyday concerns of farmers who shared intimate details with our research team as they continued to cultivate traditional cultivars, enacting in-situ conservation in the process.

The first concerns everyday hypotheses that were perceived and described over time concerning agrichemicals. While there is no "going back" to the systems of milpa farming practiced before the Green Revolution in El Salvador, there is ample reason to worry about the everyday agrichemical exposures that lead Chalateco farmers to ask researchers whether the chemicals are killing people. These concerns could directly inform investigations in environmental health concerning the role that cumulative agrichemical mixture exposures have on subsistence farmers who may or may not be correctly identified as having early life experiences with milpa farming. They should also inform methods of retrospectively assessing aggregate and cumulative agrichemical exposures among farmers who are dying too early. This may be done by developing behavioral instruments that enhance recall by using ethnographically informed anchors (as we tried to illustrate in chapter 4), and/or by inspiring approaches that leverage new and emerging assessment technologies to develop proxies for measuring aggregate and cumulative agrichemical exposures (and insults to organs) over the lifespan. The human-chemical interactions that were sometimes viewed by farmers as breaches in human-plant relations arose from a curiosity about what those chemicals, which were ubiquitous in farmers' lifeways, were doing to the humans assembled with them. We are particularly concerned with their potentially toxic effects on the people who are intimately entangled with the milpa, who may take too many agrichemical "hits" over the passage of their lifespans.

This book has offered some methodological innovations, grounded in ethnographic observation, that may be directly informative to investigations concerning the environmental health of subsistence farmers in El Salvador, and migrants from El Salvador who farmed milpas earlier in life.

In direct relation to the first concern raised above comes the second: the act of eating and rendering recipes from traditional cultivars raised by farmers who practice in-situ conservation. In our analysis of gastronomic extractivism, we employed lenses of vicarious intimacy and in-situ conservation to examine how traditional cultivars were being extracted and consumed in various environments. Ultimately, one wonders what would entail a more socially responsible way of eating or simply representing traditional cultivars outside of agrarian lifeways, particularly as their cultivators face economic poverty, the threat of chronic kidney disease of unknown origin, and pesticide poisonings. Serena Cosgrove's (2020) notion of decolonial intersectionality helped us to think through the positionality of the eater of traditional cultivars, their distance from milpas and the people who farm them, and the survival of traditional varieties. We encourage cooks and eaters of haute traditional cuisine to not de-people the experience of extracting plant material from the milpa, even though peopling the experience may involve more innovative and strategic solutions from those who may profit from or enjoy haute traditional cuisine on a Saturday night. Professor of the history of consciousness Donna Haraway (2016, 127) warns that the act of visiting can be "more than a little risky." If you choose to visit with and eat the three sisters, plant materials derived from an assemblage that likely gave rise to more-than-human intimacies, you inherit the risk of peopling the plant materials you are eating. This could lead to multiple forms of Indigenous survivance that have yet to be effectively leveraged in the burgeoning world of Salvadoran gastronomy.

Global Concerns, Local Places

This study relied on an inductive ethos to collect data and produce text, and our findings can be considered as not being driven by, but relevant to, global concerns. The Convention on Biological Diversity promotes activities applied to farmers supporting biodiversity in farmed landscapes, maintaining genetic diversity of cultivated plants, and minimizing genetic erosion (Secretariat on the Convention of Biological Diversity 2020). The decline in biodiversity throughout the Americas, coupled with the United Nations' emphasis on the value of Indigenous knowledge, make El Salvador a peculiar case. The lack of recorded history of the milpa (described in chapter 1) is emphasized by El Salvador being one of only two Central American countries (Nicaragua being the other) without a quantitative estimate of Indigenous landholdings today (IPBES 2018). El Salvador currently has <1% of its current tropical dry forest under protection and is one of the countries with the lowest rates of protection in Central America (Portillo-Quintero and Sánchez-Azofeifa 2010). While agricultural expansion poses a threat of deforestation in El Salvador, subsistence farmers continue to practice hybridized fire and fallow/agrichemical methods that sometimes burn down too much forest. The same fire-burning farmers, the ones who on the ground may be perceived as those who act against conservation efforts, are often the farmers who are engaging in everyday acts of agrobiodiversity conservation without even knowing that it is a priority to agencies or something written about by experts in reports. Most farmers who were interviewed or followed throughout their acts of in-situ conservation represented in this book are not resisting a monolithic force nor are they cooperating in collective unity to save the environment. Many of the farmers interviewed in this book are practicing something that is meaningful to them personally and to the people in networks in which they are embedded. They grow delicious food, tell affectively charged stories, and are the keepers of heirloom seeds. Many are sharply observant, innovative, and inquisitive—qualities they have had to cultivate to effectively farm milpas each year. Milpa farmers remember and long for varieties of the past, farmers have ways of sensing their milpas, and their connection as cultivators within networks of humans who long for these varieties contribute to the seeds returning each year to the milpa. Seeds need to be retained to promote agrobiodiversity, but so much of the act of conservation is achieved through open pollination in everyday lifeways rather than in underfunded state-run institutions or well-funded demonstration projects. There are investments and interventions that could be taken to better facilitate the everyday in-situ conservation efforts of Salvadoran subsistence farmers. Given that Salvadoran milpa farmers practice in-situ conservation despite a lack of programs or economic incentives says something about their effectiveness at implementing conservation—even as they are blamed for acting against conservation efforts whenever a fire burns down a section of forest.

A top-down approach will always have an inherent appeal to the outsider coming in, to the ethnographer who conducts a thorough literature review preceding fieldwork, and to the deductive thinker who is interested in testing or modifying a preexisting theory. This current book does not speak against or discourage such approaches, but it provides an alternative approach based on inductive ways of knowing that can complement such endeavors. Inductive ways of knowing should not be forgotten or sidelined as programs and logic models are developed, incentives deployed, and targets met. Top-down approaches that aim to deploy or to find the *global* in the *local* also risk ignoring how it is that so much in-situ conservation gets done in the absence of international agreements and government programs, and academics to evaluate them. Here we highlight more-than-human intimacies as an emergent property of more-than-human assemblages that, in part, drive the reproduction of Salvadoran milpa farming over time spans where volcanic eruptions, colonialism, and civil war threaten the practice. More-than-human intimacies are integral to the ongoingness of the milpa, even though they may be the stuff of subjectivity and ineffability.

Summary

In conclusion, this book was about more-than-human intimacies on Chalateca milpas and the unexpected turns taken as those intimacies were further explored. Some of these turns were methodological in nature. We approached the concepts and methods within this book by thinking with processes of returning and re-turning. Year after year, traditional cultivars have found their way back to the ground through rural Salvadorans at the margins who receive no government incentives to put them there. Rural Salvadorans enact in-situ conservation through intimate relations with nonhumans, returning the soil to recreate the milpa—an agricultural phenomenon that has survived environmental catastrophe, colonial contact, the genocide and ethnocides of its cultivators, and persistent marginalization. Year after year, farmers continue to conserve traditional cultivars in-situ, and they do so with intimate attention to the three sisters that have been the subjects of stories for centuries. This is made possible, in part, through more-than-human intimacies that keep milpa farming alive.

ACKNOWLEDGMENTS

This work was made possible by many people and nonhumans who came into contact with the authors, particularly between 2017 and 2023.

We are thankful to the team of volunteer data collectors from UCA El Salvador who traveled to and administered questionnaires in Chalatenango: Milton Alexander Escobar Arteaga, Diana Stephannie España Estrada, Edith Aída González Guevara, Josselyn Beatriz Cruz Abarca, Carlos Daniel Fernández Castro, Rodrigo José Castellanos Arévalo, Daniela Fernanda Murcia González, and Graciela Yaneth López Castillo. They worked under the guidance of Miguel Geovanny Arias Rodas, who diligently organized and managed the team, and who also contributed directly to the questionnaire, literature reviews, and editing of tables presented in the final text. We would also like to thank Fabiola Esmeralda Rubio Hernández for her support in conducting archival and literature reviews. A special thanks to Nelson Fernando Chacón Serrano for collecting qualitative interview data and contributing to our thinking on postmemory, and to Christian Villanueva for introducing us to machine learning algorithms.

Terese Gagnon and Irina Carlota Silber reviewed and provided detailed feedback on an earlier draft of the manuscript. Both also provided years of intellectual input as this work was in its formative stages. Terese Gagnon repeatedly guided the authors toward relevant literature that is cited throughout the work. Irina Carlota Silber was generous with her time, mentoring, and friendship to Mike as this book was being written, and constantly provided the intellectual guidance to hold space for a complex analysis, one that did not "de-people" as it simultaneously re-turned the nonhuman. Molly Todd pushed our thinking in chapter 5 by asking us to delve deeper into our analysis of the embroideries, providing us with references, pointing us toward Chilean arpilleras, providing new analytic considerations, and offering numerous iterations of feedback as the chapter was developed. Jeffrey Thiele, a Fulbright student grantee and doctoral student, conducted extensive editing of the text and meticulously managed dozens of files and permissions forms that facilitated the completion of the final book.

We are especially thankful to the editors of the biodiversity in small spaces series at the University of Arizona Press. Virginia Nazarea provided conceptual guidance, organized meetings and sessions that facilitated the development of concepts presented in this book, and gave the authors the encouragement over the years (and pandemic) that it took to see this work through to its fruition. Allyson Carter was especially instrumental at multiple stages of the book's development and publication, and we are thankful to her commitment and patience over the numerous years it took to complete this project. Theresa Winchell provided a careful and thoughtful edit of the final draft. Valentina Perveri provided feedback on an earlier draft of the book proposal, and we are thankful for her insights and collegiality.

As we wrote, we encountered scholars, friends, and colleagues who were generous with their time, thoughts, and connections. We are indebted to the generosity, openness of spirit, and intellect of Dr. Madeleine Scammel, who patiently took the time to repeatedly speak with Mike about the complexities of studying chronic kidney disease of unknown origin. She substantially deepened the thinking that is presented in chapter 4. Laura Kubzansky pointed us toward psychological literature on autobiographical memory that strengthened our ability to articulate arguments in chapter 4. We are thankful to Cristian Alexis Baires Moreno for helping to clarify terms and helping Mike locate "lost" recipes, and for pointing his attention to the poetry of Alfredo Espino. We are also thankful to Maria Cecilia Moreno for taking the time to prepare delicious, outstanding recipes including chachama and quesadilla de maíz. Laura cooked for Mike, tolerated him asking questions while dirtying her kitchen, and provided us with her killer recipe for torrejas with chilate. We are grateful for our entanglements with the brilliant Caroline Lacey, who generated connections in the contemporary Salvadoran art scene and who introduced Elena and Mike to one another. We are indebted to contemporary Salvadoran artists Efraín Caravantes, Wilber Salguero, and Muriel Hasbun who took ample time to explain their art, re-turn ideas, and push the horizons of the boundaries with which we see multiple worlds. We are thankful to Carlos Henríquez Consalvi (Santiago) for his hospitality and willingness to explain and share images of the embroideries housed at the Museo de la Palabra y la Imagen. Susana Portillo was instrumental in helping us navigate CENTA. We would also like to thank doña Epifanía Tepas from the *Casa de la cultura de Nahuizalco* for talking with us about her memories of the Neshtihual, Mashashte, and Nishtamal herbs that were once used to produce dyes for traditional *petates* (mats) and which have since been lost with the introduction of herbicides to the milpas, and for sharing details from her personal life.

Mike would personally like to thank the farmers who befriended him, spent time with him, and who welcomed him into their lives. His 2018–19 U.S. Fulbright Scholar grant helped to facilitate much of the data collection for this book, and publication of the book was made possible in part by funding from the Southwest Health Equity Research Collaborative at Northern Arizona University (U54MD012388), which is sponsored by the National Institute on Minority Health and Health Disparities (NIMHD). He is personally thankful to the graduate students in a grounded theory seminar he taught at UCA El Salvador, and to Amparo Marroquín Parducci, Carlos Ferrufino, and Jorge Molina Aguilar for helping him think through rhizomes in the Salvadoran context. Serena Cosgrove provided a guest lecture in the seminar and has been a friend and integral colleague ever since. He is thankful to Diana Hernandez for her mentoring in straddling social science and public health, and to the Harvard-JPB Environmental Health fellows (and the fellowship itself) for providing him with endless intellectual stimulation, encouragement, and friendship. He is thankful to his mother, Carol Wheeler, who helped him learn to sew as he began working with the first iteration of the analyses of the embroideries produced by Elena in chapter 5. Mike's *chuchas aguacateras*, Dusty and Canela, made a pandemic-era journey from El Salvador to live with him permanently in the United States, always sleeping by his desk as he wrote.

Elena would like to thank the Museo de la Palabra y la Imagen in San Salvador for working with us to access and understand the embroideries in chapter 5. To *Delicias de las Chacón* in Santa Tecla for gifting us with pastries, cebada, and an intimate sharing of Romero stories. Finally, she would like to thank her grandmother Rosa Elena Martínez (1931–2017) and great grandmother María del Carmen Mancía (1904–1992).

Elizabeth would like to thank the Institute of Current World Affairs, which funded her travel and research, especially Rebecca Picard, Joel Millman, and Amelia Frank-Vitale. Elizabeth also wanted to thank her writing teachers Tara Hardy, Christine Hemp, and Sonya Lea. In El Salvador, Jeanne Rikkers and Pablo Gabriel García Rikkers. And her in-laws, la familia Sanchez, especially Aunt Blanqui, who makes tamales with such cariño, and her favorite dinner date Eder Jacovic Campos Sánchez.

APPENDIX

Quantitative Analyses

Random forest (RF) algorithms can be used to identify variables that have high variable importance for a given dependent variable of interest (Guo et al. 2010; Hastie, Tibshirani, and Friedman 2009; Winham et al. 2012). The quantitative variables in these analyses that represent intimacies with nonhuman actants were represented as dichotomous variables (e.g., the respondent missed corn = 1 or did not miss corn = 0; the respondent dreamed about the milpa = 1 or did not dream about the milpa = 0).

RFs use recursive binary splitting to grow a tree on training data by segmenting the feature space into regions that minimize the classification error. RFs build decorrelated trees and average them, yielding a single consensus prediction (Hastie, Tibshirani, and Friedman 2009). The high variance produced by tree-based methods can be reduced with bagging (bootstrap aggregation). RFs can also accommodate a large number of predictor variables (Winham et al. 2012). For each intimacy variable that was explored in this analysis, five hundred trees were developed with p variables tried at each node/split of a given tree. Variable importance measures (VIMs) were calculated for each predictor and used as a screening tool to rank and prioritize variables for subsequent follow-up.

Deciding how to split a node can be accomplished through various approaches. For this analysis, the Gini Index was used to evaluate which variable to split at a given node, and to help identify variables for importance. The Gini Index is defined as

$$G = \sum_{k=1}^{K} \hat{p}_{mk}(1 - \hat{p}_{mk})$$

where $\hat{p}_{mk}$ represents the proportion of observations in the mth region from the kth class (Hastie, Tibshirani, and Friedman 2009). For example, if among farmers <25 years of age, the proportion of farmers who dreamed of corn was 0.90, G = 0.09. Alternatively, if we split age groups differently and the resulting proportion who dreamed of corn was 0.6, G = 0.24. The smaller G shows more node purity when age is split at 25 years of age. The node purity measure is a measure of the total decrease in node impurity that results from splits over that variable, averaged over all trees. For any given variable, the sum of the impurity decrease averaged over all trees in the forest can be used to rank variables by importance.

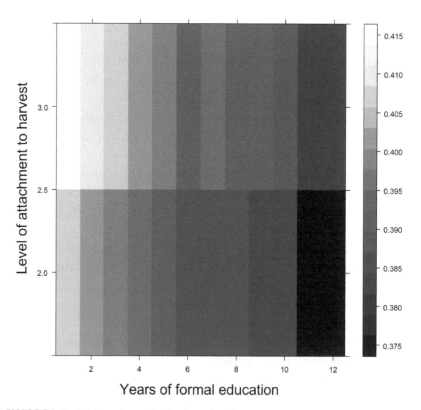

FIGURE 7.1 Partial dependence plot for dreaming about corn, in relation to years of formal education and level of attachment to the harvest. Results derived from random forests for dreaming about corn.

Relative to a given dependent variable (such as longing for corn), all the other variables in the data could then be ranked based on their overall level of importance. For any one intimacy variable, let r = importance rank. Across multiple RFs for multiple intimacy variables V, the mean rank was calculated for variables that appeared across different RF algorithms:

$$mean\ importance\ rank = \frac{1}{V}\sum_{i=1}^{V} r_i.$$

This was done to isolate the most important variables that appeared throughout different RF algorithms for different intimacy variables. Logistic regression was then used to aid in interpretation for variables with appreciable VIMs in both forests that were developed. The quantitative findings

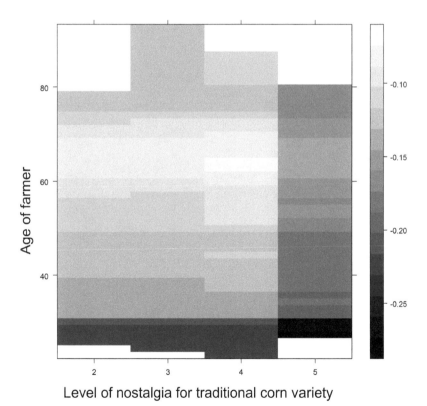

FIGURE 7.2 Partial dependence plot for in-situ conservation of a traditional corn variety, in relation to age of the farmer and level of nostalgia for traditional corn varieties. Results derived from random forests for practicing in-situ conservation of a traditional corn variety.

are generally narrated in chapter 3, but quantitative results can also be interpreted using the figures below.

To examine interaction effects in the data, lowess curves, logistic regression, and partial dependence plots derived from the RF algorithms were used to gain a better understanding of how variables might interact. Partial dependence plots for select variables covered in chapter 3 are illustrated. These include plots for dreaming about corn (figure 7.1) and in-situ conservation of a traditional corn variety (figure 7.2).

REFERENCES

Alas López, Adriana A. 2021. "El Valor de las Memorias: La Negociación Intergeneracional del Proyecto Insurgente en la Posguerra Salvadoreña." PhD diss., Colegio de Michoacán.

Alfaro de Hidalgo, Juana Celia. 2014. "Impacto Económico de las Intoxicaciones con Plaguicidas Sintéticos de Uso Agrícola, en el Municipio de San Juan Opico Departamento de La Libertad." Master's thesis, Universidad de El Salvador. https://ri.ues.edu.sv/id/eprint/7528/.

Amaroli, Paul. 1991. "Linderos y Geografía Económica de Cuscatlán, Provincia Pipil del Territorio de El Salvador." *Mesoamérica* 12 (21): 41–70.

Amaroli, Paul, and Robert Dull. 1998. "Milpas Prehispánicas en El Salvador." Paper presented at the XII Simposio de Investigaciones Arqueológicas en Guatemala, Guatemala.

Anastario, Michael, Olivia Ceavers, Paula Firemoon, Nezahualcoyotl Xiuhtecutli, and Ana Maria Rodriguez. 2022b. "Retrospective Assessment of Human-Chemical Interactions in Health-Disparity Populations: A Process Evaluation of Life History Calendars." *International Journal of Environmental Research and Public Health* 19 (19): 12397. https://doi.org/10.3390/ijerph191912397.

Anastario, Michael, Elizabeth Rink, Gitte Adler Reimer, and Malory Peterson. 2021a. "More-than-Human Intimacies and Traditional Knowledge Among Hunting Families in Northwest Greenland." *Arctic Anthropology* 58, no. 1 (June): 54–65. https://doi.org/10.3368/aa.58.1.54.

Anastario, Mike. 2019. *Parcels: Memories of Salvadoran Migration*. New Brunswick, N.J.: Rutgers University Press.

Anastario, Mike, Miguel Geovanny Arias Rodas, Milton Alexander Escobar Arteaga, Christian Villanueva, Fernando Chacón Serrano, and Hope Ferdowsian. 2021b. "Genitourinary Systems Entangled with Shifting Environments in a Salvadoran

Subsistence Farming Community." *Medical Anthropology Quarterly* 35, no. 2 (June): 246–65. https://doi.org/10.1111/maq.12616.

Anastario, Mike, Ana Maria Rodriguez, Nezahualcoyotl Xiuhtecutli, and Eric Wagner. 2022a. "Characterization of Lifetime Agrichemical Exposure Sequences Relative to International Migration in Foreign Born Latinx Agricultural Workers Living in South Florida." *Journal of Immigrant and Minority Health* 24, no. 5 (October): 1145–53. https://doi.org/10.1007/s10903-021-01278-5.

Anderson, Matthew C., Robert A. Bjork, and Elizabeth L. Bjork. 1994. "Remembering Can Cause Forgetting: Retrieval Dynamics in Long-Term Memory." *Journal of Experimental Psychology: Learning, Memory, and Cognition* 20, no. 5 (September): 1063–87. https://doi.org/10.1037//0278-7393.20.5.1063.

Arias Rodas, Miguel Geovanny. 2019. "Hibridez Cultural en el Campesinado dedicado al Maíz en Chalatenango mediante la Diáspora en Estados Unidos" [Cultural hybridity among campesinos dedicated to corn cultivation in Chalatenango through the U.S. diaspora]. Undergraduate thesis. Universidad Centroamericana Jose Simeón Cañas.

Athuraliya, Nimmi T. C., Tilak D. J. Abeysekera, Priyanie H. Amerasinghe, Ranjit Kumarasiri, Palitha Bandara, Upul Karunaratne, Abul H. Milton, and Alison L. Jones. 2011. "Uncertain Etiologies of Proteinuric-Chronic Kidney Disease in Rural Sri Lanka." *Kidney International* 80, no. 11 (December): 1212–21. https://doi.org/10.1038/ki.2011.258.

Babich, Remy, Jake C. Ulrich, E. M. Dilini V. Ekanayake, Andrey Massarsky, P. Mangala C. S. De Silva, Pathmalal M. Manage, Brian P. Jackson, et al. 2020. "Kidney Developmental Effects of Metal-Herbicide Mixtures: Implications for Chronic Kidney Disease of Unknown Etiology." *Environment International* 144 (November): 106019. https://doi.org/10.1016/j.envint.2020.106019.

Barad, Karen. 2014. "Diffracting Diffraction: Cutting Together-Apart." *Parallax* 20, no. 3 (July): 168–87. https://doi.org/10.1080/13534645.2014.927623.

Barad, Karen. 2017. "Troubling Time/s and Ecologies of Nothingness: Re-Turning, Re-Membering, and Facing the Incalculable." *New Formations* 2017, no. 9 (September): 56–86. https://doi.org/10.3898/NEWF:92.05.2017.

Belli, Robert F. 1998. "The Structure of Autobiographical Memory and the Event History Calendar: Potential Improvements in the Quality of Retrospective Reports in Surveys." *Memory* 6 (4): 383–406. https://doi.org/10.1080/741942610.

Bennett, Jane. 2010. *Vibrant Matter: A Political Ecology of Things*. Durham, N.C.: Duke University Press.

Boas, Franz. 1998. *Franz Boas Among the Inuit of Baffin Island, 1883–1884: Journals and Letters*. Edited by Ludger Müller-Wille. Translated by William Barr. Toronto: University of Toronto Press.

Borlaug, Norman E., Oddvar Aresvik, Ignacio Narvaez, and R. Glenn Anderson. 1969. "A Green Revolution Yields a Golden Harvest." *Columbia Journal of World Business* 4:9–19.

Boym, Svetlana. 2001. *The Future of Nostalgia*. New York: Basic Books.

Braidotti, Rosi. 2010. "The Politics of 'Life Itself' and New Ways of Dying." In *New Materialisms: Ontology, Agency, and Politics*, edited by Diana Coole and Samantha Frost, 201–18. Durham, N.C.: Duke University Press.

Brooks, Daniel R., Oriana Ramirez-Rubio, and Juan Jose Amador. 2012. "CKD in Central America: A Hot Issue." *American Journal of Kidney Diseases* 59, no. 4 (April): 481–84. https://doi.org/10.1053/j.ajkd.2012.01.005.

Brown, Linda A., and Andrea I. Gerstle. 2002. "Structure 10: Feasting and Village Festivals." In *Before the Volcano Erupted: The Ancient Cerén Village in Central America*, edited by Payson Sheets, 97–103. Austin: University of Texas Press.

Browning, David. 1971. *El Salvador: Landscape and Society*. Oxford: Clarendon Press.

Browning, David. 1987. *El Salvador. La Tierra y el Hombre*. 3rd ed. San Salvador: Dirección de Publicaciones.

Bryan-Wilson, Julia. 2017. *Fray: Art + Textile Politics*. Chicago: University of Chicago Press.

Bubandt, Nils, Astrid Oberborbeck Andersen, and Rachel Cypher, eds. 2022. *Rubber Boots Methods for the Anthropocene: Doing Fieldwork in Multispecies Worlds*. Minneapolis: University of Minnesota Press.

Caravantes, Efraín. 2020. "Casa." In *Juegos Florales: Volumen 47*, edited by the Ministry of Culture of El Salvador. San Salvador: Ministry of Culture of El Salvador.

Castro, Clinton. 2022. "Just Machines." *Public Affairs Quarterly* 36, no. 2 (April): 163–83. https://doi.org/10.5406/21520542.36.2.04.

Castro, Clinton, David O'Brien, and Ben Schwan. 2023. "Egalitarian Machine Learning." *Res Publica* 29 (June): 237–64. https://doi.org/10.1007/s11158-022-09561-4.

CENTA (Centro Nacional de Tecnología Agropecuaria y Forestal). "Enrique Álvarez Córdova." 2010. *Colecta de Germoplasma Criollo de Maíz, Frijol y Sorgo a Mivel Nacional*. Prepared by the CENTA Banco de Germoplasma. Ciudad Arce, El Salvador.

CENTA. "Enrique Álvarez Córdova." 2015. Gobierno de El Salvador. https://www.centa.gob.sv/2015/historia/. Webpage discontinued.

Chacón Serrano, Fernando. 2017. "Construcción de Memorias Sobre el Conflicto Armado de El Salvador en Jóvenes de una Comunidad Desplazada." Master's thesis, Universidad de Chile. https://repositorio.uchile.cl/handle/2250/167721.

Chacón Serrano, Fernando, Leslie Gómez, and Thelma Alas. 2013. "Configuración de Imaginarios Sociales Sobre la Migración Irregular en Jóvenes Potenciales Migrantes y Retornados." *Revista Estudios Centroamericanos* 68 (735): 511–43.

Chao, Sophie. 2022. *In the Shadow of the Palms: More-Than-Human Becomings in West Papua*. Durham, N.C.: Duke University Press.

Charmaz, Kathy. 2014. *Constructing Grounded Theory*. 2nd ed. London: Sage.

Clements, Charles. 1984. *Witness to War: An American Doctor in El Salvador*. Bantam Paperback ed., New York: Bantam Books.

Conlon, Catherine, Virpi Timonen, Catherine Elliott-O'Dare, Sorcha O'Keeffe, and Geraldine Foley. 2020. "Confused About Theoretical Sampling? Engaging Theoretical Sampling in Diverse Grounded Theory Studies." *Qualitative Health Research* 30, no. 6 (May): 947–59. https://doi.org/10.1177/1049732319899139.

Connell, Raewyn. 2003. *Masculinidades*. 1st ed. in Spanish. Translated by Irene Artigas and Isabel Vericat. Mexico City: Universidad Nacional Autónoma de México.

Conway, Martin A., and Christopher W. Pleydell-Pearce. 2000. "The Construction of Autobiographical Memories in the Self-Memory System." *Psychological Review* 107 (2): 261–88. https://doi.org/10.1037/0033-295X.107.2.261.

Coole, Diana H., and Samantha Frost, eds. 2010. *New Materialisms: Ontology, Agency, and Politics*. Durham, N.C.: Duke University Press.

Cornwell, Benjamin. 2015. *Social Sequence Analysis: Methods and Applications*. New York: Cambridge University Press.

Cortez, Beatriz. 2018. "La Memoria de Las Plantas: Sobre el Devenir Atmósfera." *Realidad*, no. 152, 113–24. https://doi.org/10.5377/realidad.v0i152.7785.

Cosgrove, Serena. 2010. *Leadership from the Margins: Women and Civil Society Organizations in Argentina, Chile, and El Salvador*. New Brunswick, N.J.: Rutgers University Press.

Cosgrove, Serena. 2020. "Framing: Decolonial Intersectionality." In *Surviving the Americas: Garifuna Persistence from Nicaragua to New York City*, edited by José Idiáquez, 32–44. Cincinnati, Ohio: University of Cincinnati Press.

Cytowic, Richard E. 2018. *Synesthesia*. Cambridge, Mass.: MIT Press.

DeLanda, Manuel. 2006. *A New Philosophy of Society: Assemblage Theory and Social Complexity*. London: Continuum.

Dull, Robert A. 2007. "Evidence for Forest Clearance, Agriculture, and Human-Induced Erosion in Precolumbian El Salvador." *Annals of the Association of American Geographers* 97, no. 1 (March): 127–41. https://doi.org/10.1111/j.1467-8306.2007.00527.x.

Dull, Robert A., John R. Southon, and Payson Sheets. 2001. "Volcanism, Ecology and Culture: A Reassessment of the Volcán Ilopango TBJ Eruption in the Southern Maya Realm." *Latin American antiquity* 12, no. 1 (March): 25–44. https://doi.org/10.2307/971755.

Engel, Lawrence S., Matthew C. Keifer, Mary Lou Thompson, and Shelia H. Zahm. 2001. "Test-Retest Reliability of an Icon/Calendar-Based Questionnaire Used to Assess Occupational History." *American Journal of Industrial Medicine* 40, no. 5 (November): 512–22. https://doi.org/10.1002/ajim.1119.

Engel, Lawrence S., Matthew C. Keifer, and Shelia H. Zahm. 2001. "Comparison of a Traditional Questionnaire with an Icon/Calendar-Based Questionnaire to Assess Occupational History." *American Journal of Industrial Medicine* 40, no. 5 (November): 502–11. https://doi.org/10.1002/ajim.1118.

Erickson, Bonnie H. 1979. "Some Problems of Inference from Chain Data." *Sociological Methodology* 10:276–302. https://doi.org/10.2307/270774.

Erquicia Cruz, José Heriberto, and Martha Marielba Herrera Reina. 2014. *Historia, Patrimonio e Identidades en el Municipio de Comasagua, La Libertad, El Salvador*. San Salvador: La Universidad Tecnológica de El Salvador.

Espino, Alfredo. 1996. *Jícaras Tristes*. San Salvador: Consejo Nacional para la Cultura y el Arte.

Falkowski, Tomasz B., Adolfo Chankin, Stewart A. W. Diemont, and Robert W. Pedian. 2019. "More Than Just Corn and Calories: A Comprehensive Assessment of the Yield and Nutritional Content of a Traditional Lacandon Maya Milpa." *Food Security* 11, no. 2 (March): 389–404. https://doi.org/10.1007/s12571-019 -00901-6.

Ford, Anabel, and Ronald Nigh. 2015. *The Maya Forest Garden: Eight Millenia of Sustainable Cultivation of the Tropical Woodlands*. Walnut Creek, Calif.: Left Coast Press.

Foucault, Michel. 1980. "Truth and Power." In *Power/Knowledge: Selected Interviews and Other Writings 1972–1977*. Edited by Colin Gordon. Translated by Colin Gordon, Leo Marshall, John Mepham, and Kate Soper, 109–33. New York: Pantheon Books.

Freedman, Deborah, Arland Thornton, Donald Camburn, Duane Alwin, and Linda Young-DeMarco. 1988. "The Life History Calendar: A Technique for Collecting Retrospective Data." *Sociological Methodology* 18:37–68. https://doi.org/10.2307 /271044.

Fuentes, Cecilia. 2020. "El Salvador, el segundo país en el mundo con la cuarentena más larga." *ElSalvador.com*. June 8, 2020. https://www.elsalvador.com/noticias /nacional/el-salvador-segundo-pais-cuarentena-mas-larga/722164/2020/.

Gallo-Ruiz, Lyanne, Caryn M. Sennett, Mauricio Sánchez-Delgado, Ana García-Urbina, Tania Gámez-Altamirano, Komal Basra, Rebecca L. Laws, et al. 2019. "Prevalence and Risk Factors for CKD Among Brickmaking Workers in La Paz Centro, Nicaragua." *American Journal of Kidney Diseases* 74, no. 2 (August): 239–47. https://doi.org/10.1053/j.ajkd.2019.01.017.

Gay y Blasco, Paloma, and Liria de la Cruz Hernández. 2012. "Friendship, Anthropology." *Anthropology and Humanism* 37, no. 1 (June): 1–14. https://doi.org/10.1111 /j.1548-1409.2012.01104.x.

Glasner, Tina J., and Wander van der Vaart. 2009. "Applications of Calendar Instruments in Social Surveys: A Review." *Quality and Quantity* 43, no. 3 (May): 333–49. https://doi.org/10.1007%2Fs11135-007-9129-8.

González, Roberto J. 2001. *Zapotec Science: Farming and Food in the Northern Sierra of Oaxaca*. Austin: University of Texas Press.

Gordon, Avery. 2008. *Ghostly Matters: Haunting and the Sociological Imagination*. Minneapolis: University of Minnesota Press.

Gould, Jeffrey L., and Aldo Lauria-Santiago. 2008. *1932, Rebelión en la Oscuridad*. San Salvador: Museo de la Palabra y la Imagen.

Graeber, David. 2004. *Fragments of an Anarchist Anthropology*. Chicago: Prickly Paradigm Press.

Grosfoguel, Ramon. 2013. "The Structure of Knowledge in Westernized Universities: Epistemic Racism/Sexism and the Four Genocides/Epistemicides of the Long 16th Century." *Human Architecture* 11, no. 1 (Fall): 73–90.

Gunatilake, Sarath, Stephanie Seneff, and Laura Orlando. 2019. "Glyphosate's Synergistic Toxicity in Combination with Other Factors as a Cause of Chronic Kidney Disease of Unknown Origin." *International Journal of Environmental Research and Public Health* 16, no. 15 (July): 2734. https://doi.org/10.3390/ijerph 16152734.

Guo, Yu, Armin Graber, Robert N. McBurney, and Raji Balasubramanian. 2010. "Sample Size and Statistical Power Considerations in High-Dimensionality Data Settings: A Comparative Study of Classification Algorithms." *BMC Bioinformatics* 11, no. 1 (September): 447. https://doi.org/10.1186/1471-2105-11-447.

Guthman, Julie. 2019. *Wilted: Pathogens, Chemicals, and the Fragile Future of the Strawberry Industry*. Oakland: University of California Press.

Halberstam, Jack/Judith. 2011. *The Queer Art of Failure*. Durham, N.C.: Duke University Press.

Hall, Budd L., and Rajesh Tandon. 2017. "Decolonization of Knowledge, Epistemicide, Participatory Research and Higher Education." *Research for All* 1, no. 1 (January): 6–19. https://doi.org/10.18546/RFA.01.1.02.

Haraway, Donna J. 2016. *Staying with the Trouble: Making Kin in the Chthulucene*. Durham, N.C.: Duke University Press.

Haraway, Donna, Anna Tsing, and Gregg Mitman. 2019. "Reflections on the Plantationocene: A Conversation with Donna Haraway and Anna Tsing, Moderated by Gregg Mitman." *Edge Effects Magazine*. June 18, 2019. https://edgeeffects.net /wp-content/uploads/2019/06/PlantationoceneReflections_Haraway_Tsing.pdf.

Harrison, Peter. 2007. "Maya Agriculture." In *Maya: Divine Kings of the Rain Forest*, edited by Nikolai Grube. Königswinter: H. F. Ullmann.

Hartigan, John, Jr. 2017. *Care of the Species: Races of Corn and the Science of Plant Biodiversity*. Minneapolis: University of Minnesota Press.

Hartman, Carl V. 2001. "Reconocimiento Etnográfico de los Aztecas de El Salvador." *Mesomaérica* 22 (41): 146–91.

Hasbun, Muriel. 2016. "Santos y Sombras Saints and Shadows." *ReVista* 15, no. 3 (Spring): 90–91.

Hastie, Trevor, Robert Tibshirani, and Jerome Friedman. 2009. "Random Forests." In *The Elements of Statistical Learning Data Mining, Inference, and Prediction*. 2nd ed., 587–603. New York: Springer.

Hecht, Susanna B., and Sassan S. Saatchi. 2007. "Globalization and Forest Resurgence: Changes in Forest Cover in El Salvador." *BioScience* 57, no. 8 (September): 663–72. https://doi.org/10.1641/B570806.

Heckathorn, Douglas D. 2002. "Respondent-Driven Sampling II: Deriving Valid Population Estimates from Chain-Referral Samples of Hidden Populations." *Social Problems* 49, no. 1 (February): 11–34. https://doi.org/10.1525/sp.2002 .49.1.11.

Heidenry, Rachel. 2014. "The Murals of El Salvador: Reconstruction, Historical Memory and Whitewashing." *Public Art Dialogue* 4, no. 1 (April): 122–45. https://doi .org/10.1080/21502552.2014.878486.

Hernández Rivas, Annette Georgina. 2015. "Cartografía de la Memoria: Actores, Lugares, Prácticas en El Salvador de Posguerra (1992–2015)" PhD diss., Universidad Autónoma de Madrid. https://repositorio.uam.es/handle/10486/672117.

Herrera-Valdés, Raúl, Carlos M. Orantes Navarro, Miguel Almaguer, Pedro Alfonso, Héctor D. Bayarre, Irma M. Leiva, Magaly J. Smith, et al. 2014. "Clinical Characteristics of Chronic Kidney Disease of Nontraditional Causes in Salvadoran Farming Communities." *MEDICC Review* 16, no. 2 (April): 39–48. https://doi.org/10.37757/MR2014.V16.N2.7.

Hetherington, Kregg. 2020. *The Government of Beans: Regulating Life in the Age of Monocrops.* Durham, N.C.: Duke University Press.

Hirsch, Marianne. 2012. *The Generation of Postmemory: Writing and Visual Culture After the Holocaust.* New York: Columbia University Press.

Hirsch, Marianne, and Leo Spitzer. 2006. "What's Wrong with This Picture? Archival Photographs in Contemporary Narratives." *Journal of Modern Jewish Studies* 5 (2): 229–52. https://doi.org/10.1080/14725880600741615.

hooks, bell. 2015. *Black Looks: Race and Representation.* New York: Routledge.

IPBES (Intergovernmental Science-Policy Platform on Biodiversity and Ecosystem Services). 2018. *The IPBES Regional Assessment Report on Biodiversity and Ecosystem Services for the Americas.* Edited by Jake Rice, Cristiana Simão Seixas, María Elena Zaccagnini, Mauricio Bedoya-Gaitán, and Natalia Valderrama. Bonn: IPBES Secretariat. https://doi.org/10.5281/zenodo.3236253.

IPBES. 2019. *Global Assessment Report on Biodiversity and Ecosystem Services of the Intergovernmental Science-Policy Platform on Biodiversity and Ecosystem Services.* Edited by Eduardo S. Brondizio, Josef Settele, Sandra Díaz, and Hien T. Ngo. Bonn: IPBES Secretariat. https://doi.org/10.5281/zenodo.3831673.

Jackson, John L. 2013. *Thin Description: Ethnography and the African Hebrew Israelites of Jerusalem.* Cambridge, Mass.: Harvard University Press.

Jansen, Kees. 1998. *Political Ecology, Mountain Agriculture, and Knowledge in Honduras.* Amsterdam: Thela Publishers.

Jayasumana, Channa, Priyani Paranagama, Suneth Agampodi, Chinthaka Wijewardane, Sarath Gunatilake, and Sisira Siribaddana. 2015. "Drinking Well Water and Occupational Exposure to Herbicides is Associated with Chronic Kidney Disease, in Padavi-Sripura, Sri Lanka." *Environmental Health* 14:6. https://doi.org/10.1186/1476-069X-14-6.

Johnson, Richard J., Catharina Wesseling, and Lee S. Newman. 2019. "Chronic Kidney Disease of Unknown Cause in Agricultural Communities." *New England Journal of Medicine* 380, no. 19 (May): 1843–52. https://doi.org/10.1056/NEJMra1813869.

Kantor, Hayden S. 2019. "A Body Set Between Hot and Cold: Everyday Sensory Labor and Attunement in an Indian Village." *Food, Culture and Society* 22, no. 2 (March): 237–52. https://doi.org/10.1080/15528014.2019.1573045.

Kantor, Hayden S. 2020. "Locating the Farmer: Ideologies of Agricultural Labor in Bihar, India." *Anthropology of Work Review* 41, no. 2 (Winter): 97–107. https://doi.org/10.1111/awr.12208.

Kim, Su-ji, Hyo-Wook Gil, Jong-Oh Yang, Eun-Young Lee, and Sae-Yong Hong. 2009. "The Clinical Features of Acute Kidney Injury in Patients with Acute Paraquat Intoxication." *Nephrology, Dialysis, Transplantation* 24, no. 4 (April): 1226–32. https://doi.org/10.1093/ndt/gfn615.

Kirksey, Eben. 2015. *Emergent Ecologies.* Durham, N.C.: Duke University Press.

Latour, Bruno. 2005. *Reassembling the Social: An Introduction to Actor-Network Theory.* Oxford: Oxford University Press.

Law, John, and Marianne Lien. 2018. "Denaturalizing Nature." In *A World of Many Worlds,* edited by Marisol de la Cadena and Mario Blaser, 131–71. Durham, N.C.: Duke University Press.

Laws, Rebecca L., Daniel R. Brooks, Juan José Amador, Daniel E. Weiner, James S. Kaufman, Oriana Ramírez-Rubio, Alejandro Riefkohl, et al. 2015. "Changes in Kidney Function Among Nicaraguan Sugarcane Workers." *International Journal of Occupational and Environmental Health* 21, no. 3 (January): 241–50. https://doi.org/10.1179/2049396714Y.0000000102.

Lebov, Jill F., Lawrence S. Engel, David Richardson, Susan L. Hogan, Jane A. Hoppin, and Dale P. Sandler. 2016. "Pesticide Use and Risk of End-Stage Renal Disease Among Licensed Pesticide Applicators in the Agricultural Health Study." *Occupational and Environmental Medicine* 73 (1): 3–12. https://doi.org/10.1136/oemed-2014-102615.

Lebov, Jill F., Lawrence S. Engel, David Richardson, Susan L. Hogan, Dale P. Sandler, and Jane A. Hoppin. 2015. "Pesticide Exposure and End-Stage Renal Disease Risk Among Wives of Pesticide Applicators in the Agricultural Health Study." *Environmental Research* 143, pt. A (November): 198–210. https://doi.org/10.1016/j.envres.2015.10.002.

Lentz, David L., and Carlos R. Ramírez-Sosa. 2002. "Cerén Plant Resources: Abundance and Diversity." In *Before the Volcano Erupted: The Ancient Cerén Village in Central America,* edited by Payson Sheets, 33–42. Austin: University of Texas Press.

Lindo, Héctor. 2015. "El proceso económico." In *Historia contemporánea de El Salvador,* edited by Carlos Gregorio López Bernal, 201–65. San Salvador: Fundación MAPFRE and Editorial Universitaria.

Lopez-Ridaura, Santiago, Luis Barba-Escoto, Cristian A. Reyna-Ramirez, Carlos Sum, Natalia Palacios-Rojas, and Bruno Gerard. 2021. "Maize Intercropping in the Milpa System. Diversity, Extent and Importance for Nutritional Security in the Western Highlands of Guatemala." *Scientific Reports* 11, no. 1 (February): 3696. https://doi.org/10.1038/s41598-021-82784-2.

Martín-Cleary, Catalina, and Alberto Ortiz. 2014. "CKD Hotspots Around the World: Where, Why and What the Lessons Are; A CKJ Review Series." *Clinical Kidney Journal* 7, no. 6 (December): 519–23. https://doi.org/10.1093/ckj/sfu118.

Martínez Lara, Carlos Benjamín. 2016. *Memoria Histórica del Movimiento Campesino de Chalatenango.* San Salvador: UCA Editores.

McClean, Michael, Rebecca Laws, Oriana Ramirez Rubio, and Daniel Brooks. 2010. *Industrial Hygiene/Occupational Health Assessment: Evaluating Potential Hazards Associated with Chemicals and Work Practices at the Ingenio San Antonio (Chichigalpa, Nicaragua)*. Boston: Boston University School of Public Health.

McReynolds, Samuel A. 2002. "Land Reform in El Salvador and the Chapultepec Peace Accord." *Journal of Peasant Studies* 30, no. 1 (January 1): 135–69.

Mendley, Susan R., Adeera Levin, Ricardo Correa-Rotter, Bonnie R. Joubert, Elizabeth A. Whelan, Brian Curwin, Erik H. Koritzinsky, et al. 2019. "Chronic Kidney Diseases in Agricultural Communities: Report from a Workshop." *Kidney International* 96, no. 5 (November): 1071–76. https://doi.org/10.1016/j.kint.2019.06.024.

Menjívar, Cecilia, and Néstor Rodríguez, eds. 2005. *When States Kill: Latin America, the U.S., and Technologies of Terror*. Austin: University of Texas Press.

Mesnage, Robin, Nicolas Defarge, Joël Spiroux de Vendômois, and Gilles-Eric Séralini. 2015. "Potential Toxic Effects of Glyphosate and Its Commercial Formulations Below Regulatory Limits." *Food and Chemical Toxicology* 84:133–53. https://doi.org/10.1016/j.fct.2015.08.012.

Miller, Gary W. 2020. *The Exposome: A New Paradigm for the Environment and Health*. 2nd ed. London: Academic Press.

Miller, Gary W., and Dean P. Jones. 2014. "The Nature of Nurture: Refining the Definition of the Exposome." *Toxicological Sciences* 137, no. 1 (January): 1–2. https://doi.org/10.1093/toxsci/kft251.

Mistral, Gabriela. 2008. *Madwomen: The Locas Mujeres Poems of Gabriela Mistral*. Edited and translated by Randall Couch. Chicago: University of Chicago Press. A bilingual edition.

Molina, Jorge. 2022. *Pedagogías de la Muerte*. San Salvador: Editorial Universidad Don Bosco and Editorial El Venado Blanco.

Monge, Patricia, Catharina Wesseling, Jorge Guardado, Ingvar Lundberg, Anders Ahlbom, Kenneth P. Cantor, Elisabete Weiderpass, and Timo Partanen. 2007. "Parental Occupational Exposure to Pesticides and the Risk of Childhood Leukemia in Costa Rica." *Scandinavian Journal of Work, Environment and Health* 33, no. 4 (August): 293–303. https://doi.org/10.5271/sjweh.1146.

MSPAS (Ministerio de Salud Pública y Asistencia Social). 1999. *Memoria del II Foro Nacional de Plaguicidas Propuestas de Prohibición de Productos Altamente Tóxicos en El Salvador*. Organización Panamericana de la Salud/Organización Mundial de la Salud, El Salvador.

MSPAS. 2000a. *Intoxicaciones por Plaguicidas 1999–2000 El Salvador*.

MSPAS. 2000b. *Memoria del I Foro Nacional de Comités Locales del Proyecto de PLAGSALUD*. Organización Panamericana de la Salud/Organización Mundial de la Salud, El Salvador.

Münster, Daniel. 2022. "Plants of Internal Colonization: Critical Descriptions of Agrarian Change Through Plant Agencies in South India." In *Rubber Boots Methods for the Anthropocene: Doing Fieldwork in Multispecies Worlds*, edited by Nils

Bubandt, Astrid Oberborbeck Andersen, and Rachel Cypher, 119–45. Minneapolis: University of Minnesota Press.

MUPI (Museo de la Palabra y la Imagen). 2019. *Colección Bordadoras de Memorias.* University of Texas at Austin Latin American Digital Initiatives. https://ladi-prod.lib.utexas.edu/es/mupi03.

Nazarea, Virginia D. 1998. *Cultural Memory and Biodiversity.* Tucson: University of Arizona Press.

Nazarea, Virginia D. 2005. *Heirloom Seeds and Their Keepers: Marginality and Memory in the Conservation of Biological Diversity.* Tucson: University of Arizona Press.

Nazarea, Virginia D. 2014. "Potato Eyes: Positivism Meets Poetry in Food Systems Research." *Culture, Agriculture, Food and the Environment* 36, no. 1 (June): 4–7. https://doi.org/10.1111/cuag.12024.

Nixon, Rob. 2011. *Slow Violence and the Environmentalism of the Poor.* Cambridge, Mass.: Harvard University Press.

Nyamongo, Isaac K. 2002. "Assessing Intracultural Variability Statistically Using Data on Malaria Perceptions in Gusii, Kenya." *Field Methods* 14, no. 2 (May): 148–60. https://doi.org/10.1177/1525822X02014002002.

Olson, David M., Eric Dinerstein, Eric D. Wikramanayake, Neil D. Burgess, George V. N. Powell, Emma C. Underwood, Jennifer A. D'amico, et al. 2001. "Terrestrial Ecoregions of the World: A New Map of Life on Earth." *BioScience* 51, no. 11 (November): 933–38. https://doi.org/10.1641/0006-3568(2001)051[0933:TEOTWA]2.0.CO;2.

Orantes Navarro, Carlos M., Raúl Herrera-Valdés, Miguel A. Almaguer-López, Elsy G. Brizuela-Díaz, Lilian Núñez, Nelly P. Alvarado-Ascencio, E. Jackeline Fuentes-de Morales, et al. 2014. "Epidemiology of Chronic Kidney Disease in Adults of Salvadoran Agricultural Communities." *MEDICC Review* 16, no. 2 (April): 23–30. https://doi.org/10.37757/MR2014.V16.N2.5.

Orantes Navarro, Carlos M., Raúl Herrera-Valdés, Miguel Almaguer López, Denis J. Calero, Jackeline Fuentes de Morales, Nelly P. Alvarado Ascencio, Xavier F. Vela Parada, Susana M. Zelaya Quezada, Delmy V. Granados Castro, and Patricia Orellana de Figueroa. 2015. "Epidemiological Characteristics of Chronic Kidney Disease of Non-Traditional Causes in Women of Agricultural Communities of El Salvador." *Clinical Nephrology* 83 (7): 24–31. https://doi.org/10.5414/CNP83S024.

Orellana Guevara, Luis Alonso, and Roberto Alejandro Flores Romero. 2019. "Modelos Autorregresivos Integrado de Medias Móviles (ARIMA) y Vectores Autorregresivos (VAR) Aplicados a la Producción Nacional de Maíz y Frijol en El Salvador para el Periodo 1955–2030." Master's thesis, Universidad Centroamericana José Simeón Cañas.

Oslé, Emma. 2022. "Lost and Found: Unearthing the Echoes of Muriel Hasbun's Seismic Traces." *The Latinx Project* (blog), *Center for Women in the Arts and Humanities, Rutgers University.* April 5, 2022. https://www.latinxproject.nyu.edu/intervenxions/lost-and-found-unearthing-the-echoes-of-muriel-hasbuns-seismic-traces.

PAHO (Pan American Health Organization). 2002. "Demographic and Mortality Trends in the Region of the Americas, 1980–2000." *Epidemiological Bulletin* 23, no. 3 (September). https://www3.paho.org/english/sha/be_v23n3-editorial2 .htm.

Pearce, Jenny. 1986. *Promised Land: Peasant Rebellion in Chalatenango, El Salvador.* London: Latin America Bureau.

Peraza, Sandra, Catharina Wesseling, Aurora Aragon, Ricardo Leiva, Ramón Antonio García-Trabanino, Cecilia Torres, Kristina Jakobsson, Carl Gustaf Elinder, and Christer Hogstedt. 2012. "Decreased Kidney Function Among Agricultural Workers in El Salvador." *American Journal of Kidney Diseases* 59, no. 4 (April): 531–40. https://doi.org/10.1053/j.ajkd.2011.11.039.

Pérez Brignoli, Héctor. 1995. "Indians, Communists, and Peasants: The 1932 Rebellion in El Salvador." In *Coffee, Society, and Power in Latin America*, edited by William Roseberry, Lowell Gudmundson, and Mario Samper Kutschbach, 232–61. Baltimore: Johns Hopkins University Press.

Peveri, Valentina. 2020. *The Edible Gardens of Ethiopia: An Ethnographic Journey into Beauty and Hunger.* Tucson: University of Arizona Press.

Phillips, Ronald L. 2013. "Norman Ernest Borlaug: 25 March 1914–12 September 2009." *Biographical Memoirs of Fellows of the Royal Society* 59:59–72. https://doi .org/10.1098/rsbm.2013.0012.

Pizzigoni, Caterina. 2007. "Region and Subregion in Central Mexican Ethnohistory: The Toluca Valley, 1650–1760." *Colonial Latin American Review* 16, no. 1 (June): 71–92. https://doi.org/10.1080/10609160701336063.

Portillo-Quintero, Carlos A., and Gerardo A. Sánchez-Azofeifa. 2010. "Extent and Conservation of Tropical Dry Forests in the Americas." *Biological Conservation* 143, no. 1 (January): 144–55. https://doi.org/10.1016/j.biocon.2009.09.020.

Pugliese, Joseph. 2020. *Biopolitics of the More-Than-Human: Forensic Ecologies of Violence.* Durham, N.C.: Duke University Press.

Quandt, Sara A., Dana C. Mora, Theresa L. Seering, Haiying Chen, Thomas A. Arcury, and Paul J. Laurienti. 2020. "Using Life History Calendars to Estimate in Utero and Early Life Pesticide Exposure of Latinx Children in Farmworker Families." *International Journal of Environmental Research and Public Health* 17 (10): 3478. https://doi.org/10.3390/ijerph17103478.

Raffles, Hugh. 2020. *The Book of Unconformities: Speculations on Lost Time.* New York: Pantheon Books.

Reber, Vera Blinn. 1978. "Art as a Source for the Study of Central America, 1945–1975: An Exploratory Essay." *Latin American Research Review* 13 (1): 39–64. https://doi .org/10.1017/S0023879100030673.

Roberts, Elizabeth F. S. 2019. "Bioethnography and the Birth Cohort: A Method for Making New Kinds of Anthropological Knowledge about Transmission (Which Is What Anthropology Has Been about All Along)." *Somatosphere.* November 19, 2019. http://somatosphere.net/2019/bioethnography-anthropological-knowledge -transmission.html/.

Roberts, Elizabeth F. S. 2021. "Making Better Numbers Through Bioethnographic Collaboration." *American Anthropologist* 123, no. 2 (June): 355–69. https://doi .org/10.1111/aman.13560.

Roberts, Elizabeth F. S., and Camilo Sanz. 2018. "Bioethnography: A How-to Guide for the Twenty-First Century." In *The Palgrave Handbook of Biology and Society*, edited by Maurizio Meloni, John Cromby, Des Fitzgerald, and Stephanie Lloyd, 749–75. London: Palgrave Macmillan.

Rockefeller Foundation. n.d. "Edwin J. (Edwin John) Wellhausen." Online Collection and Catalog of Rockefeller Archive Center. Accessed April 13, 2020. https://dimes .rockarch.org/agents/4A4yock3m4yjuUpLTybE4w?category=&limit=40&query= Edwin%20wellhausen.

Rodríguez, Teresa, Berna van Wendel de Joode, Christian H. Lindh, Marianela Rojas, Ingvar Lundberg, and Catharina Wesseling. 2012. "Assessment of Long-Term and Recent Pesticide Exposure Among Rural School Children in Nicaragua." *Occupational and Environmental Medicine* 69 (2): 119–25. https://doi.org/10.1136/oem .2010.062539.

Romero, Óscar A., Jon Sobrino, Ignacio Martín-Baró, and Rodolfo Cardenal. 1980. *La Voz de los Sin Voz: la Palabra Viva de Monseñor Oscar Arnulfo Romero*. San Salvador: UCA Editores.

Roncal-Jimenez, Carlos, Miguel A. Lanaspa, Thomas Jensen, Laura Gabriela Sanchez-Lozada, and Richard J. Johnson. 2015. "Mechanisms by Which Dehydration May Lead to Chronic Kidney Disease." *Annals of Nutrition and Metabolism* 66, no. 3 (June): 10–13. https://doi.org/10.1159/000381239.

Ross, Norbert, Tomás Barrientos, and Alberto Esquit-Choy. 2005. "Triad Tasks, a Multipurpose Tool to Elicit Similarity Judgments: The Case of Tzotzil Maya Plant Taxonomy." *Field Methods* 17 (3): 269–82. https://doi.org/10.1177/1525822X05277861.

Salamanca, Elena. 2015. "Es la Cumbia la que Manda en mi País." *Landsmoder* (blog), *El Faro*. July 21, 2015. https://losblogs.elfaro.net/landsmorder/2015/07/es-la -cumbia-la-que-manda-en-mi-pa%C3%ADs.html.

Salamanca, Elena. 2017. *Clásicos de la Pintura Salvadoreña*. San Salvador: Universidad Pedagógica de El Salvador.

Salguero, Wilber. 2022. *Hombre de Maíz // Serie*. San Salvador, El Salvador.

Sammells, Clare A. 2019. "Reimagining Bolivian Cuisine: Haute Traditional Food and Its Discontents." *Food and Foodways* 27, no. 4 (October): 338–52. https://doi.org /10.1080/07409710.2019.1677396.

Sanford, Victoria. 2003. *Buried Secrets: Truth and Human Rights in Guatemala*. New York: Palgrave Macmillan.

Scammell, Madeleine K., Caryn M. Sennett, Zoe E. Petropoulos, Jeanne Kamal, and James S. Kaufman. 2019. "Environmental and Occupational Exposures in Kidney Disease." *Seminars in Nephrology* 39, no. 3 (May): 230–43. https://doi.org/10.1016 /j.semnephrol.2019.02.001.

Secretariat of the Convention of Biological Diversity. 2020. *Global Biodiversity Outlook 5*. Montreal. https://www.cbd.int/gbo5.

Sellen, Adam. 2011. "Sowing the Blood with the Maize: Zapotec Effigy Vessels and Agricultural Ritual." *Ancient Mesoamerica* 22, no. 1 (October): 71–89. https://doi .org/10.1017/S0956536111000095.

Sheets, Payson D., ed. 1983. *Archeology and Volcanism in Central America: The Zapotitán Valley of El Salvador.* Austin: University of Texas Press.

Sheets, Payson D., ed. 2002. *Before the Volcano Erupted: The Ancient Cerén Village in Central America.* Austin: University of Texas Press.

Sheets, Payson, and Michelle Woodward. 2002. "Cultivating Biodiversity: Milpas, Gardens, and the Classic Period Landscape." In *Before the Volcano Erupted: The Ancient Cerén Village in Central America,* edited by Payson Sheets, 184–91. Austin: University of Texas Press.

Shiva, Vandana. 2016. *Stolen Harvest: The Hijacking of the Global Food Supply.* Lexington: University Press of Kentucky.

Silber, Irina Carlota. 2007. "Local Capacity Building in 'Dysfunctional' Times: Internationals, Revolutionaries, and Activism in Postwar El Salvador." *Women's Studies Quarterly* 35, no. 3/4 (Fall/Winter): 167–83.

Silber, Irina Carlota. 2010. *Everyday Revolutionaries: Gender, Violence, and Disillusionment in Postwar El Salvador.* New Brunswick, N.J.: Rutgers University Press.

Silber, Irina Carlota. 2022. *After Stories: Transnational Intimacies of Postwar El Salvador.* Redwood City, Calif.: Stanford University Press.

Simmel, Georg. 1955. *Conflict and the Web of Group-Affiliations,* translated by Kurt H. Wolff and Reinhard Bendix. New York: Free Press.

Smith, Linda Tuhiwai. 2012. *Decolonizing Methodologies: Research and Indigenous Peoples.* 2nd ed. London: Zed Books.

Smith, Terry. 2019. *Art to Come: Histories of Contemporary Art.* Durham, N.C.: Duke University Press.

Stengers, Isabelle. 2018. "The Challenge of Ontological Politics." In *A World of Many Worlds,* edited by Marisol de la Cadena and Mario Blaser, 83–111. Durham, N.C.: Duke University Press.

Strathern, Marilyn. 2004a. *Partial Connections.* Lanham, Md.: Rowman & Littlefield.

Strathern, Marilyn. 2004b. *Commons and Borderlands: Working Papers on Interdisciplinarity, Accountability and the Flow of Knowledge.* Wantage, U.K.: Sean Kingston.

Sutton, David E. 2001. *Remembrance of Repasts: An Anthropology of Food and Memory.* Oxford: Berg.

Taube, Karl Andreas. 1989. "A Classic Maya Entomological Observation." In *Studies in Ancient Mesoamerican Art and Architecture: Selected Works,* 168–73. San Francisco: Precolumbia Mesoweb Press. https://www.mesoweb.com/publications /Works1/Taube_Works_v1.pdf.

Tedlock, Dennis. 1996. *Popol Vuh: The Definitive Edition of the Mayan Book of the Dawn of Life and the Glories of Gods and Kings.* New York: Simon & Schuster.

Tilley, Virginia. 2005. *Seeing Indians: A Study of Race, Nation, and Power in El Salvador.* Albuquerque: University of New Mexico Press.

Todd, Molly. 2010a. *Beyond Displacement: Campesinos, Refugees, and Collective Action in the Salvadoran Civil War*. Madison: University of Wisconsin Press.

Todd, Molly. 2010b. "Remapping the Tierra Olvidada." In *Beyond Displacement: Campesinos, Refugees, and Collective Action in the Salvadoran Civil War*, 15–49. Madison: University of Wisconsin Press.

Todd, Molly. 2021a. *Long Journey to Justice: El Salvador, the United States, and Struggles Against Empire*. Madison: University of Wisconsin Press.

Todd, Molly. 2021b. "This Promised Land." In *Long Journey to Justice: El Salvador, the United States, and Struggles Against Empire*, 138–78. Madison: University of Wisconsin Press.

Tousignant, Noémi. 2018. *Edges of Exposure: Toxicology and the Problem of Capacity in Postcolonial Senegal*. Durham, N.C.: Duke University Press.

Tsing, Anna Lowenhaupt. 2015. *The Mushroom at the End of the World: On the Possibility of Life in Capitalist Ruins*. Princeton, N.J.: Princeton University Press.

Unión Rural de Productores de Cuautempan y Tetela. 2021. "La Dobla, una Práctica Milenaria que está Potenciando la Disponibilidad de Maíz." *Centro Internacional de Mejoramiento de Maíz y Trigo*. https://idp.cimmyt.org/la-dobla-una-practica-milenaria-que-esta-potenciando-la-disponibilidad-de-maiz/.

Valcke, Mathieu, Marie-Eve Levasseur, Agnes Soares da Silva, and Catharina Wesseling. 2017. "Pesticide Exposures and Chronic Kidney Disease of Unknown Etiology: An Epidemiologic Review." *Environmental Health* 16:49. https://doi.org/10.1186/s12940-017-0254-0.

Vega Trejo, Ana L., Kevin Rivera, Elena Salamanca, Donovan Najarro, Carlos Aguiluz, Lissette de Schilling, and Nelson Crisóstomo. 2019. *45 Años del Banco de Fomento Agropecuario Entretejiendo Vidas e Historia*. San Salvador: Banco de Fomento Agropecuario.

Verran, Helen. 2018. "The Politics of Working Cosmologies Together While Keeping Them Separate." In *A World of Many Worlds*, edited by Marisol de La Cadena and Mario Blaser, 112–30. Durham, N.C.: Duke University Press.

Vikrant, Sanjay. "Hepato-Renal Toxicity-Associated with Methyl Parathion Exposure." 2015. *Renal Failure* 37 (2): 355–56. https://doi.org/10.3109/0886022X.2014.986620.

Vinebaum, Lisa. 2020. "The Subversive Stitch Revisited." In *A Companion to Textile Culture*, 275–97. Hoboken, N.J.: John Wiley. https://doi.org/10.1002/9781118768730.ch15.

Wanderer, Emily. 2020. *The Life of a Pest: An Ethnography of Biological Invasion in Mexico*. Berkeley: University of California Press.

Wellhausen, Edwin. 1990. "Algunas Reflexiones sobre el PCCMCA." *Agronomia Mesoamericana* 1 (1): 97–106. https://dialnet.unirioja.es/servlet/articulo?codigo=5529981.

Wild, Christopher Paul. 2005. "Complementing the Genome with an 'Exposome': The Outstanding Challenge of Environmental Exposure Measurement in Molecular Epidemiology." *Cancer Epidemiology, Biomarkers and Prevention* 14, no. 8 (August): 1847–50. https://doi.org/10.1158/1055-9965.EPI-05-0456.

Williams, Robert G. 1986. *Export Agriculture and the Crisis in Central America.* Chapel Hill: University of North Carolina Press.

Winham, Stacey J., Colin L. Colby, Robert R. Freimuth, Xin Wang, Mariza de Andrade, Marianne Huebner, and Joanna M. Biernacka. 2012. "SNP Interaction Detection with Random Forests in High-Dimensional Genetic Data." *BMC Bioinformatics* 13, no. 1 (July): 164. https://doi.org/10.1186/1471-2105-13-164.

Zahm, Shelia Hoar, Joanne S. Colt, Lawrence S. Engel, Matthew C. Keifer, Andrew J. Alvarado, Keith Burau, Patricia Butterfield, et al. 2001. "Development of a Life Events/Icon Calendar Questionnaire to Ascertain Occupational Histories and Other Characteristics of Migrant Farmworkers." *American Journal of Industrial Medicine* 40, no. 5 (November): 490–501. https://doi.org/10.1002/ajim.1117.

INDEX

Note: Page numbers in *italics* refer to illustrative matter.

ABOUT THE AUTHORS

Michael Anastario is an assistant professor of health sciences at Northern Arizona University. A former Fulbright Scholar to El Salvador and Harvard-JPB Environmental Health Fellow, he is the author of *Parcels: Memories of Salvadoran Migration*. Anastario's research interests concern rural health disparities and the science of harm reduction.

Elena Salamanca is a Salvadoran writer and historian currently pursuing a PhD in history at El Colegio de Mexico. She teaches at the National Autonomous University of Mexico and has published poetry and fiction, including *Tal vez monstruous, Prudencia Ayala: La niña con pájaros en la cabeza*, and *Claudia Lars: La niña que vio una salamandra*.

Elizabeth Hawkins is a San Salvador-based attorney and writer with a background in representing immigrants and asylum seekers. A recipient of the Critchfield fellowship from the Institute of Current World Affairs, Hawkins focuses her research on access to justice, gender-based violence, intergenerational trauma, and women's post-pandemic recovery in El Salvador.